INDIAN MUTINY
AND BEYOND

Robert Haydon Shebbeare VC

INDIAN MUTINY AND BEYOND

The Letters of Robert Shebbeare VC

Edited by Arthur Littlewood

Pen & Sword
MILITARY

First published in Great Britain in 2007 by
Pen & Sword Military
an imprint of
Pen & Sword Books Ltd
47 Church Street
Barnsley
South Yorkshire
S70 2AS

ISBN 978-1-84415-574-3

A CIP catalogue record for this book is
available from the British Library.

Typeset in 11/13pt Sabon by
Concept, Huddersfield, West Yorkshire

Printed and bound in England by
Biddles Ltd

For a complete list of Pen & Sword titles please contact
PEN & SWORD BOOKS LIMITED
47 Church Street, Barnsley, South Yorkshire, S70 2AS, England
E-mail: enquiries@pen-and-sword.co.uk
Website: www.pen-and-sword.co.uk

CONTENTS

For the Shebbeares,
and for Victoria, with love.

ACKNOWLEDGEMENTS

Robert Shebbeare, great-nephew of Robert Shebbeare VC, for the pleasure of our collaboration and for his advice on many subjects.

Mary Lamb, née Shebbeare, great-niece, for kindly giving access to family papers.

The National Army Museum, Chelsea, for the excellent help given by the staff in the Reading Room; and for permission to use the extract from a letter from Colonel Kendal Coghill.

Professor N. Burgess, formerly of the Royal Defence Medical College, Millbank, London, for advice on medical matters.

The photographs of India and China were sent home to the family by Robert Shebbeare.

The British Library, for the help given by the library staff at the Oriental and India Record Office.

John Govett, great-great-nephew, kindly created the family tree and afforded me much help and information.

The Centre of South Asian Studies, Cambridge University, for kind permission to use extracts from the Coghill Papers and for their help in my research.

The authors listed in the bibliography, many of them long dead, who have given me some understanding of the period. Of particular mention is Saul David, whose recent and scholarly book, *The Indian Mutiny, 1857*, was of invaluable help in preparing the Introduction to Chapter Two.

David Cole of Digital Colour Services at Hedgerow Print, Crediton, for his technical help.

The engraving from the *Illustrated London News* 1860 is reproduced by permission of the Syndics of Cambridge University Library.

GLOSSARY

Badmash	bandit
Batta	an allowance for service outside India, or for service in war.
Cantonment	permanent military station.
Chapatti, chupatti	thin unleavened biscuit.
Dak, dawk	transport system for post or carriage of people, by relays of men, horses and bullocks.
Deg	lidded vessel for food, something like a billycan.
Gharry	small, enclosed horse-drawn carriage.
Ghee	clarified butter for cooking.
Havildar	Indian non-commissioned officer, equivalent to sergeant, hence havildar major.
Jemadar	junior Indian officer.
Lota, lotah	brass drinking pot, used by high-caste Indians.
Moonshie, munshi	interpreter, clerk.
Mufti	civilian (non-uniform) clothing.
Naik	Indian equivalent to corporal.
Palanquin	covered litter carried on poles.
Pathan	Muslim from borders of Afghanistan and present-day Pakistan.
Poorbea, purbia	soldiers from north Indian region from which the majority of sepoys were recruited (Oudh, Benares and Bihar).
Posteen	winter coat of sheepskin (or other animal skin) with fleece worn inside.

Pugrie, puggree	muslin scarf around hat and sometimes falling behind the neck as protection against the sun.
Pukka, pucka	proper.
Rupee	silver coin, in 1850s valued at one tenth of a pound sterling.
Sepoy	private soldier in the Indian Army.
Serai	a building for travellers, with a courtyard and often fortified. Sometimes a palace or harem (hence 'seraglio'). The serai in Kissengunge is noted as a 'mosque' by Robert Shebbeare.
Sowar	cavalry trooper in Indian army.
Subedar, subadar	senior Indian officer.

INTRODUCTION

In 2004, following the death of his brother, Major J.D. Shebbeare, my friend Robert Inge Shebbeare, for whom macular degeneration has made reading difficult, asked me to help him to go through his family papers with him. It became, and still is, a very absorbing occupation, for the many collections of letters over three centuries comprise a fascinating document of social life seen through the eyes of one family.

Quite early on, we came across a letter headed 'Camp before Delhi', and dated 11 July 1857. On reading it through it at once became apparent that this was a very exciting account of events during the Indian Mutiny. Robert then said that his great-uncle, Robert Haydon Shebbeare, who won his Victoria Cross at the assault on Delhi, had written letters home to various members of the family, and that he had a few more at home himself, as well as some other correspondence of that time.

In all, it turned out that there were some thirty-seven letters from Robert Shebbeare that had survived, spread over the course of his military life, plus others from well-known personalities involved in the siege of Delhi. His letters were obviously circulated amongst his family at the time, as they exist as originals, copies hand-written at the time, type-written transcripts and, in a few cases, as photocopies of letters whose whereabouts are not known.

Robert Shebbeare's life was moulded by the traditions, values and constraints of a particular era and his letters home during a long exile from England reflect attitudes of that time, a few of which may seem rather alien in today's non-colonial culture. He was by all accounts an intelligent and likeable young man with a good sense of humour, so it is easy to identify with the everyday happenings and problems he encountered during his life as a soldier. He became, in the opinion of his contemporaries, a gifted leader and his shrewd observations on the military events and the personalities of the day bring to life many well-known incidents during the Indian Mutiny. Pride in his regiment, quiet patriotism and a love of his family at home all sustained him in his long stay abroad, and managed to keep him with his ideals intact in the face of the intense heat, acute boredom, bureaucratic annoyances and increasing homesickness that often tended to sap the energies of Europeans in the tropics.

In 1844, he left England at the age of seventeen and served for sixteen years as a regimental officer, in India and China, during which time he never again saw his family, nor was he able to take home leave.

He died at sea, aged thirty-three, while returning to England on extended sick leave. His whole family was waiting in welcome at the quayside when his ship docked at Tilbury, only to be told that his body had been buried at sea off the coast of China.

At one level this is a sad and tragic story, and one which no doubt haunted the members of a close family for the rest of their lives. In reading his letters, however, one becomes aware that the life he led as a soldier was for him a very fulfilling one. Despite the hardships and discomforts, not to mention the extreme danger on many occasions, Robert Shebbeare was happy and content in the friendships and camaraderie of his regimental life – perhaps he would not have wished for a retirement with its vista of declining years, had he managed to attain it.

The Indian Mutiny of 1857 has always held a fascination to those many people interested in both social and military history and there is already a copious body of literature which deals with the complex reasons which led to it, as well as recording the exciting and often tragic events which took place during that turbulent period. There are many first-hand accounts written by soldiers and politicians of the time and each, although it may be coloured by a particular and subjective viewpoint, adds something to this enormous topic. Memoirs written long afterwards have a tendency to cast the writer in flattering terms which are not necessarily shared by contemporaries, while certain aspects of a situation are sometimes distorted or filtered out in order to enhance the writer's viewpoint. In doing the research for this, it has been remarkable to find how many different, and sometimes even contradictory, descriptions there are of any single event, and how much influence the interaction of personalities can have on the course of history.

The letters are published without omissions for two reasons. Firstly, the manner of writing often gives clues as to Robert Shebbeare's state of mind at the time, and secondly, in doing the research for this, I have found that small snippets of useful information are constantly cropping up in other letters and articles – what may apparently be a piece of coal to one reader may seem a nugget of gold to another.

Each chapter begins with a short piece of very general background information to put events in context, which may be helpful to those unfamiliar with this period, at the risk of oversimplifying the many complexities of an enormous topic. There are many admirable books which cover the whole subject of the British in India and a plethora which deal with the mutiny itself, so it is not the intention of this book to do anything but provide some little vignettes to add to the considerable body of knowledge about this most interesting period.

References and occasional explanatory notes may be found at the end of each chapter. No attempt has been made to standardize the spelling of Indian place-names that are mentioned: thus Ambala may appear as Umballah, Oudh as Oude, and so on.

The intention is that the letters can be read as an interesting story in themselves, and can also be used as a source of information for research into a particular topic.

Shebbeare is a family that originated in Devon and over the generations it has produced many distinguished soldiers, sailors, lawyers and churchmen. A short family history can be found at the end of this book.

Robert Haydon Shebbeare was the son of Charles John Shebbeare, a London barrister, and his wife Louisa Matilda (née Wolfe). He had four brothers and four sisters who survived infancy, one of whom, Alice, he never saw as she was born after he left for India. His letters have passed through the family and are now with the last surviving member of a trio of Shebbeares who saw military service: William (Bill) Shebbeare, 23rd Hussars, killed leading his squadron at the Battle of Caen; John Shebbeare, Poona

Horse; and Robert Inge Shebbeare, who served with the 10th Hussars.

Robert Inge Shebbeare has kindly given many of the family papers in his possession, some dating back to 1580, to the Devon Record Office, where they should make a very interesting source of material for future historians.

The photographs of India and China in this book are by Felice Beato (1825–1903). He was a naturalized Englishman who, from 1850, worked with his brother-in-law, James Robertson and, in 1855, as pioneer war photographers, they documented the Crimean War.

Beato went to India in 1858 and took photographs of the damage done during the mutiny. Robert Shebbeare sent home an album of his 'Views of Delhi' together with other photographs.

In 1860 he followed the British Army out to China where he took photographs of people and places during the campaign, including some for his 'Indian Celebrities' series, in which Robert Shebbeare features, and of the 15th Punjab Regiment.

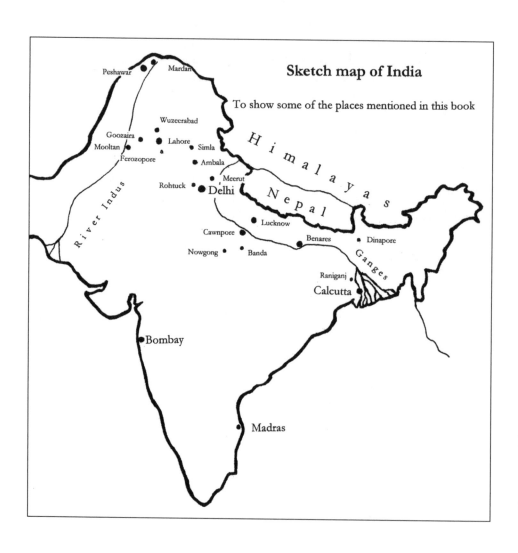

Sketch map of India

To show some of the places mentioned in this book

Chapter One

LIFE AS A YOUNG
REGIMENTAL OFFICER

In 1600, the Honourable East India Company (HEIC), known also as the John Company, was granted a charter to have a monopoly of trade in Asia; by the beginning of the eighteenth century it had expanded to become one of the most important commercial enterprises in the world, with Indian cotton as the main source of its growing prosperity, together with opium, indigo and sugar. At first, the Company relied on the goodwill of local Indian rulers to gain concessions, but once the main settlements of Bombay, Madras and Calcutta were established, British influence became more significant and the HEIC saw the need to recruit soldiers to guard its many interests. Regiments of native soldiers, or sepoys, were formed, with a small number of British officers in command. In the mid-part of the century a weakening Moghul empire broke down and many of the new states which resulted from this formed alliances with the British and French in return for trading concessions. The French were beaten at the Battle of Plassey in 1763; at about the same time, the British displaced the ruler in Bengal and governed it themselves. From that time onwards the British continued to annexe states to suit their commercial purposes, with the Company providing the administration on behalf of the British government. By the time that Robert Shebbeare arrived in India in 1844 the HEIC was a vast organization, with a large body of troops divided into the separate armies of Bombay, Madras and Bengal, the latter being by far the biggest of these.

At this time, an officer in the British Army had to purchase a commission, was expected to have private means sufficient to maintain a suitable lifestyle and was thus of necessity drawn from the better-off sections of society. Honourable East India Company officers, however, were recruited from a much wider social base, and as a consequence the education and calibre of the cadets was more mixed; many, though by no means all, were motivated more by the prospect of earning enough to enable them to attain financial security and social status than to make careers as soldiers.

The greater proportion of boys who were nominated as being suitable to become officers in the Company's armies entered via a direct cadetship, whereby they were sent out to India to join a regiment and to learn soldiering by a kind of military symbiosis, whose success was very dependent on the quality of those with whom they came in contact.

From 1840 to 1842, Robert Shebbeare had been at King's College School, which was at that time in the Strand in London, only moving at the turn of the century to Wimbledon. A younger fellow pupil at the school was Philip Salkeld, who won a posthumous Victoria Cross at the Kashmir Gate on the same day that Robert Shebbeare was awarded his.

From 1809 to 1861 a smaller number of the better-educated cadets were trained at the HEIC military college at Addiscombe near Croydon, which took teenage boys of fourteen to eighteen years of age who had been recommended by persons of standing known to the Company, and it was here that fifteen-year-old Robert went next.

From all accounts, the education was very mixed in quality and the regime was tough. The cadets were drilled and took part in other military exercises; they studied drawing, surveying and fortification, as well as learning French, Latin and Hindustani.

After this rudimentary initial training the young ensigns were sent out in one of the Company's sailing ships to India where, after a period attached to a regiment, they were given a permanent posting to a particular regiment. New arrivals from England were called 'griffins', or 'griffs', who largely learnt how things happened from their seniors.

Once the initial excitement had worn off the young officers settled into a routine that was often tedious and irksome for long periods, as most of the regiments in central India were engaged in policing, rather than military duties. Much of the time was spent in cantonments where there was little cultural or social life and for the most part recreation was taken in the company of a small group of fellow bachelors, many of whose interests were of a robust, outdoor kind, while those of an intellectual bent were usually in a minority. During the hot season in May and June, the suffocating heat confined the British within doors during the day; this was followed by the equally disagreeable rains of the monsoon. Senior officers joined administrators in escaping to the hill stations in the north at this time, while those less fortunate remained to keep things ticking over.

There were, of course, compensations and the cool season transformed the countryside into a place of immense beauty; local leave often consisted of game-hunting expeditions in spectacular scenery.

Promotion was by length of service, rather than merit, which was one of the reasons why, at the beginning of the Mutiny, so many of the senior regimental officers were found to be ill-equipped to deal with the difficulties they faced. More able officers were often seconded to civil administrative duties with better pay; and regimental duty, in the absence of campaigns which might bring prize money, had come to be seen as something to be endured rather than enjoyed. Ambitious young men were frustrated at being unable to exercise their talents and petty jealousies often led to friction between members of such an enclosed society.

Having said all that, there was within most regiments a good esprit de corps, and the camaraderie induced by shared privation and danger helped to forge many lifelong friendships, which did much to sustain men so far from home.

The letters which follow in this chapter cover Robert Shebbeare's first eleven years with his regiment, and from them one can trace his progress in a number of military cantonments where there was little military action and not too much mental stimulation. Some young officers had a network of connections when they arrived in India and, under the patronage of relations and family friends, got themselves rapidly into plum appointments. Robert had none of these advantages but he nevertheless plodded quietly along in the system, learning several Indian languages, becoming Adjutant and making lasting friendships amongst forward-looking and talented young officers. One gathers from his early letters that writing seems to be more of a duty than a particularly pleasurable activity and he is not given to many flights of literary fancy, but in many ways this is something of a virtue as he records his happenings honestly, solely to give his family some idea of what he was experiencing, as a son and as a brother, in a distant and strange land. The lack of action in battle seen by his regiment during these years must have seemed very irksome to him, for in 1853 he wrote wistfully: 'It seems fated that we shall not see any service.' Fate, however, had different plans for him, as the events of 1857 will show in due course.

Dinapore, 17th November, 1844

My dear Mother,

I did not write a letter by the last mail because I could not any how make one, having no materials at all, for everything has been going on the dawk. I am still doing duty with the 36th and am likely to be with it a month or so longer when I hope to be posted. There are now about twenty to be posted before me. I hope to be posted before they give each regiment the new Captain, which is to be in January, for if I am I shall get a step by it, whereas if the Captain is given first it will only be a post.

Tomorrow the 62nd Queens are going to have their colours presented to them. They have asked the other regiments to a ball and supper in the evening. We shall have to go to it as doing duty with the regiment, though I would much rather not as I do not know any ladies in Dinapore. I met McNiel here the other day who formerly belonged to the 36th but now is in the 5th. Is he any relation to the Rev H. McNiel? I was told he was; I suppose it could not have been Alexander McNiel. There is a great fair at a place called Hadjipore in a day or two; almost everybody is going. We have got leave to go but I do not think that I shall go except for a day. It lasts ten days or more. There are horse races and balls and dinners and all that sort of thing. It begins at the new moon when the natives come from great distances to bathe in the Ganges at that part. They believe that by bathing at the new moon exactly at that part they are also freed from their sins. It is said to be well worth seeing. It is also a large horse fair and a good place to pick up a good horse cheap.

I had a letter yesterday from Mr W. Bracken in Calcutta. I suppose by this time you are all settled at Balham Hill. I think I remember where it is, about opposite Chings the Ironmongers. I was very glad to hear that the respectable old lady had been turned out. How are the Mitcham tenants going on? Does Harry collect the rents? I have moved into quarters that are much cheaper and I now live with a griff of the name of Davidson who also came out in the Poichiers. I should have liked to be at Sandgate with you very much; it must have been very pleasant. It is the beginning of the cold weather here. Now I sleep always with a blanket and even in the middle of the day it is not too hot to go about. In the morning I am very glad to wear cloth trousers. I dare say it will be very hot at the ball this evening for the old hands, who are obliged to go in full dress, but till we have been in the country a year we have no right to wear it.

The 15th Regiment march from here tomorrow on their way to Calcutta from whence they are going to Chauk Phu in Ardean. The 62nd Queens also march in a short time to Umballah. There is a ball to be given for them before they go, so there are plenty of balls about this time.

I suppose my Father went to France. Did Harry go with him? I don't think he was much of a French scholar. I tried to talk French the other day to a man who came about begging but I could do nothing but Hindustani and English with a few words of French here and there and as he could talk Hindustani I found I could make him understand that better than my French. I still keep the Moonshie and I flatter myself that I talk better every day, tho' he told me that I was not talking very gentlemanly Hindustani the other day, but was talking like a villager, the large towns being the only places where good Hindustani is spoken. Am afraid I shall never be a good hand at writing a letter, at all events when I have no news, which is the case now, so with kind love and remembrances to yourself, my father and everybody,

believe me my dear mother,

your affectionate son,

Robert H. Shebbeare

(On same letter)

Dinapore, 18th November

My dear Peggy,

I am very much obliged and amused by your letters and should have written to you but I could not find anything amusing to tell you. However, I will write you something next time at all events. With love to Emma and Helen and also Jack, believe me your affectionate brother.

R.Shebbeare

Ferozepore, April 17th, 1849

My Dear Jack,

I received your letter this morning and proceed to answer it, as you desire. First I will answer your questions as well as I can. You will know what sort of a place I live in. I can only tell you that it is in a very hot country but I cannot tell you the exact spot for during the last six months I have had no house, but my tent or boat has been my home. I am now going to Wuzeerabad in the middle of the Sikh country. You are wrong in supposing the Sikhs are cowards for they have shown themselves brave men. The country is all quiet now. You will see Wuzeerabad marked on any large map of India, about seventy or eighty miles east of Lahore. I start directly I can get camels to carry my sepoys' beds, pans and kettles.

I am glad to hear that you get on so well with your Latin. I am learning a new language, Persian, but have not had much time for studying for the last six months. You are quite right to learn music for I recollect that you have a very good ear. I would like to be able to play the piano better than any instrument except the violin which requires so much practice as to make its study a labour. I have not played the flute for a long time but in any case I never learnt enough of music to become even a tolerable player. We have a very good band in the regiment so I hear a good deal of music when with it, but I have now been away for three months and the only music (if you can call it so) which I have heard is a screaming noise made by some of the servants, to the pleasant accompaniment of a small drum.

I had a pleasant trip up the river Sully as there were several other officers with me and I had a very nice boat. There are lots of alligators in the river and we used to see them every day basking in the sun on sandbanks. The jungles on the banks of the river contain wild boar and some few tigers, and in the river and on sandbanks in it there are large flocks of wild geese and ducks, of which we shot a good many; also pelicans, cranes and storks of various kinds, large and small.

I brought a curious dog from Bahawulpore. He is a Persian greyhound, in shape like an English greyhound covered all over the legs with long white silky hair. His ears are like a spaniel's. He was brought down by an Afghan from the Hhorasan and given me by a friend whom I met at Bahawaulpore. I think I have now told you all I can about myself. I hope you will write again.

Believe me your ever affectionate brother,

Robert H. Shebbeare

I received Mamma's letter of the 17th February in which yours was enclosed this morning. The letter of December which I answered a few days ago had been lying in the Post Office for some time.

Wuzeerabad, June 7th, 1849

My dear Charles,

Do not be afraid of sending me stale news. Any letter from home is interesting and I seldom find any repetition in those I receive. At the time you wrote you describe yourself as sitting by the fire; at that time I was endeavouring to keep myself cool in a tent at Ferozopore, but without succeeding.

I marched from Ferozopore about the 20th April and arrived here 3rd May. I found all our fellows hard at work building in order to get under cover before the hot winds set in. I was too late to think of that so I set to work to build at leisure (for as I told you before there was not a hut of any sort before our army arrived), and to live in a tent all the hot weather would be very unsafe. I am building a hut of unburnt brick, twenty-four feet long by twelve feet in breadth, flat at the top and raised about two feet from the ground as they say that water lies on the ground in the rains. I began at first to build on the most economical principles, but before it had progressed far a house built in the same style fell in, so I have been obliged to build on a more expensive scale and fear I shall not finish it under 250 Rs, a heavy pull on me in my present circumstances. However, I spend nothing on other things – my grub costs me very little and my beverage is water. Beer is a rupee a bottle here so I can't indulge in it and water I never cared about. I found it very hard to give up beer this hot weather, one requires something better than water. I have in fact given up every luxury and some things which are considered necessaries. I have no horse nor have had for some time. I have not given up tobacco nor is there any occasion to, as I can get beautiful Cavendish at one shilling a lb – so I can indulge myself with a pipe and keep a clear conscience. I cannot describe the station to you well for I have seen little of it. It is very flat and dusty, within one mile of the Chenaub. [second page missing]

A note in Riddell's 'Record of the 60th Regiment of Bengal Native Infantry'[1] records that 'Lt-Col Smith died from fatigue and exposure after the regiment were obliged to build hutments for themselves at Wuzeerabad.'

Banda, February 25th, 1852

My dear mother,

I missed last mail, being unaware of its going out until too late, and was very nearly missing this for the same reason. In fact I have never time to scribble a line for the sake of writing. I have had a great deal of work lately, being quartermaster, secretary of band and book club committee, and having acted as adjutant in the absence of the pucka adjutant for nearly a month. This was my chief reason for allowing the post to slip away without a letter. Now that I do write I can only tell you that I am quite well and happy and will send you a long letter next mail. The hot weather is now fast approaching and I suppose we shall be obliged to remain indoors all day shortly.

With love to all, believe me, dear mother,

your affectionate son, Robert H. Shebbeare

Nowgong, May 7th, 1852

My dear Emma,

I received your letter in the middle of the jungles a few days ago and as you express a wish to receive a letter addressed to yourself particularly I will endeavour to gratify you, although Charles tells me that my letters go round the family in general, for which reason I have always addressed them to my mother.

Doyne and I started from Banda on the 17th of April with a man called Passanah from Orai, with the intention, or rather the hope, of shooting tigers, in which as yet we have been signally unsuccessful. However, we make a fresh start from this station in company with a Colonel Smyth of the 3rd Cavalry who has elephants prepared and has heard of the whereabouts of several tigers, so we have yet a chance of realising a skin or two. We have had most delightful weather, quite extraordinary for this time of year – even in the tents we have not felt the heat severe at all. Nowgong is a very pretty little station, garrisoned by the 3rd Cavalry and a wing of the 55th. We have been here five days and have been very hospitably treated.

Almost all the people seem to be Irish and come from the same part as Doyne. Their brogue is something terrific. Last night we were dining with Mrs. Haig, a sister of Mrs. Riddell of our corps, and she and I were the only English people at the table, the rest (some eight or ten) were either very Irish or equally Scotch – in fact at Nowgong an Englishman appears to be a curiosity!

8

We have only ten days leave remaining and we are now starting in the opposite direction from Banda so we shall have to return to Banda in one day. The distance is about eighty miles so I shall ride half way and pay a palkie dak for the other forty as the weather is too hot to ride the whole way. I have written palkie dak but you will probably not understand; palkie means palanqueen and dak is travelling. My relays of bearers or horses are in fact relays of any conveyance. Palanqueen travelling is very tedious and very slow, four miles an hour the average, and the bearers wake one up every stage for 'buckshish', without which they will not travel an inch, notwithstanding that they receive regular pay.

I really must stop writing now as there are three or four idle fellows talking nonsense in the room and I fear I am writing equal 'twaddle'. I will write you again next mail and do better if I can.

With best love to all at home, believe me dear Joan,

your ever affectionate brother, Robert H. Shebbeare

Banda, October 18th, 1853

My dear Harry,

Since I wrote last we have received our orders to remain at Banda another year, ie the headquarters of the regiment remain and I, of course, being on the staff remain with the colours, but a wing has already marched for Nowgong, about seventy miles S.W. from Banda, to relieve the 55th and take the duties of that station until another regiment arrives from Mooltan. They will be absent altogether for about six months. I suppose that our wretched little station will be more empty than ever during the cold weather. Moreover the small numbers of officers will prevent my getting a month's leave as I had intended, which is a bore. However, as some sort of compensation the Post Office becomes vacant and I am now in addition of my other emoluments enjoying a salary of seventy rupees and the important post of Post Master at Banda. This gives me some little trouble but not enough to make it a disagreeable situation. The addition to my pay will assist materially in enabling me to polish off my debts, which work I am happy to say is going on very favourably and promises to be completed within a reasonable period. Should I be fortunate enough to obtain one of the regimental staff appointments permanently you may expect, if all goes well, to see me in England in about two years time.

I am very glad that the India Bill was passed as it did not seem desirable to introduce any very violent reforms at once and now the system is left open to reform and gradual improvements as it becomes necessary. It is very ridiculous to talk about the people of India wishing for any grand reform – the fact is that very few of them, in fact only the well educated residents in large cities who are in constant communication with Europeans, have even heard of any change taking place or have any idea of the expiration of the Charter, or what the Charter is, or indeed to go further, what 'The Company' is beyond the fact that it is a power governing them much more justly and satisfactorily than they were ever ruled by the best native princes. I have been lately reading the Indian blue book and it is astonishing what very extraordinary statements some of the officials examined are betrayed into making by cross examination. As to the information of a great part of the members who spoke on the subject in the House, it may be put down at a very small figure. Some of the misrepresentations are perfectly absurd. I could give many instances but have not the time. The fact is, it is ridiculous for a man to speak about the Government of India who has not seen it working and has not also seen native governments working alongside it. One man in Parliament (if not more) said that our Government was so oppressive that the people left our own states for those under native rule. The opposite is the fact. I could mention a thousand instances of people leaving Oude for our provinces, and many more would do so if not deterred by the dislike of leaving land which has been in their family for a long time, and they manage to carry on somehow or other, by bribing the native officers employed by the King of Oude, and by occasionally turning out under arms to resist any very serious oppression such as an attempt on the part of the local governor to collect the Revenue twice over, which frequently happens. In fact, in Oude men plough with a sword and shield at their side and a sepoy who lives in a disturbed part of that country told me that no man sits down to eat without laying his sword and shield across the threshold, to be ready in case of any disturbance. This is of course a little exaggerated but shows nevertheless the native idea of a part of the country which it was stated men fly to from our own provinces. It is very lucky that the detail of the system of government is left to be carried out in India, as it is utterly unreasonable to suppose that it could be settled by people who know nothing of the character and peculiarities of the people.

I suppose that we shall obtain what we wished in the way of new furlough regulations but I cannot say at present exactly what they will be. It seems probable that new European regiments will be raised which will give us a lift in the way of promotion, possibly two steps in this regiment. I am writing under several disadvantages.

Firstly the flies have fixed on me as a victim, apparently because they see that I am very bust! Secondly, there are about fifty tailors making sepoys' coats in the verandah and they come in constantly to show me a 'fit' – besides all this I am in a great hurry as the Post leaves at twelve o'clock and it is 'latest safe day', a fact I was not aware of when I sat down to write. I must shut up now or I shall be late.

With kindest love to my mother and all at home, believe me your affectionate brother, Robert H. Shebbeare

Wuzeerabad, November 18th, 1853

My dear Harry,

I have just received yours of the 19th September and although I do not feel much in a vein for writing, having been suffering from a dreadful cold for the last few days which makes me quite stupid, I will nevertheless give you a few lines by this mail.

The relief is out and we have orders to proceed to Cawnpore! and much to our disgust to start on the 1st February. It is fifty-six marches, I believe, so we shall not get there until after the hot winds have set in. Cawnpore is in my opinion the most disgusting station in India out and out. Very hot, very dusty and upward of five miles long, so station duty there is no joke. 'Au reste' stores are cheap enough, and house rent ought to be very low, as the number of troops quartered there has been greatly decreased, and we shall have some society at all events, all of which I have not enjoyed for some time. It is rumoured that we are to escort Shere Sing and Chutter Sing down country; I hope not as it will add so much to our duty. [Chatar Singh and his son Shere Singh had been thorns in the side of the British during the Sikh war. They were comprehensively defeated at the Battle of Gujarat in February 1849 and held captive thereafter.]

We shall again be quite out of the way in the event of war breaking out. It seems fated that we shall not see any service. I went up on the 15th and passed the interpreter's examination. I am now, as you say, at the end of my examinations, and qualified to hold any appointment. I mean to have a shy at Punjabee though, as soon as I get the grammars and dictionaries. I have subscribed to some which are advertised for publication immediately, and as there is a Punjabee regiment now at Cawnpore I hope to be able to find someone able to teach me.

I am in great hopes of selling my house. It was originally a speculation of my own but two of our officers have joined with me in

11

improving it, by pulling down the thatch of their house and putting it on to mine in the shape of a verandah. When this is finished the house will have thatched verandah on three sides and a flat roofed one on the fourth and will be worth a great deal more, as no house sells well without verandahs. They will take a quarter share of the house and we live in it until it is sold.

You enquire about my brother officers. They are mostly a very good lot, though of course we have some black sheep amongst us. There are only about twelve of us with the corps at present; however, most of them are of the best sort so we manage to amuse ourselves, notwithstanding the dullness of this station. Our present commanding officer is a most disgusting character, a sneaking, low-minded quarrelsome fellow who has been despised by the whole regiment ever since he has been in it. Luckily, being only a brevet major, he has no chance of keeping the corps long, but he has taken the opportunity of his temporary command to alter all the old regimental rules and customs for ridiculous ways of his which will last no longer than during his own reign, and give immense trouble to men and officers.[2] Add to all this that he has been some twenty-five years in the service and cannot drill a company much less the regiment, and that he seldom speaks a word of truth unless he knows that it will injure someone, and you have a correct picture of our commandant. Don't think that I am prejudiced against the man for I have no personal quarrel, but this is his character in the Army.[3]

I don't think I have much chance of a meeting with your friend in the 15th Hussars as I don't suppose they will come to our part of India. I shall be a lieutenant by the time I write to you again, as we have just bought out our major. For this step I pay Rs.980. I shall have to borrow it and pay off by giving up the difference. [Further pages missing]

Umballah, April, 1855

My dear Mother,

I am afraid I have behaved very badly in regard to letter writing of late but I really have some little excuse, for since arrival here in the beginning of January, until the camp of exercise was broken up, I scarcely had a minute that I could call my own – and since that we have been inspected by the Brigadier which has given me a great deal of work also. The camp was an imitation of the English Chobham and a very large force was assembled. We had constant field days and parades, and towards the end the Commander-in-Chief came to

Umballah and inspected us several times. The regiment I am glad to say behaved very creditably within the camp, and was reported by the Brigadier as in excellent order. All this is very pleasant as the adjutant gets credit for the appearance and the behaviour of the regiment as well as the commanding officer, although the general rule is said to be that the commanding officer takes the credit for anything creditable and gives the blame to the adjutant for everything which is the contrary!

I like our station pretty well now that I have a little time to make acquaintances. It is comparatively a new cantonment and has not very good roads. These however are improving and the houses are very good. I have been forced to buy a house, borrowing the money of course, but as I got the estate cheap I shall not be likely to lose by it even after calculating the interest on the money. I say 'forced' to buy. The fact is that the rent would have been very high and I managed to arrange to pay in instalments towards the liquidation of the loan, not much higher than my monthly rent would have been. In two years, if all goes well, the house will become my property without encumbrance. You ask regarding my speculation in carts and bullocks. It answered very well as I have been able to sell the whole stock for as much as it cost me.

Our march was not quite so pleasant to me as our former marches have been as I have had an attack of fever, rather severe, about three weeks before we left Banda, and although quite well when we started I had constant relapses all the way and was obliged to starve a good deal and give up all attempts at shooting till towards the end of the journey. I was consequently rather thin and weak on my arrival at Umballah but am thankful to be able to say that I picked up my strength again quickly and was able to go through all the work of parades etc without a day's sickness. Poor George Birch! His wife was taken ill at the commencement of the march and grew gradually weaker, till he was obliged to leave her at Delhi with some friends. He returned almost immediately after the regiment arrived here but only to find her so ill that she seldom recognised him and she died on the second day and his own death followed hers almost immediately. I have lost a great many friends lately and have indeed few left in this country; many acquaintances I of course have, but in one's absence from home and from all relations one feels a want of friends who can feel with me and take an interest in the same things, which is not the case with more everyday acquaintances.

I have got a box of pebble bracelets and little ornaments of that sort which I collected during the stay at Banda and had left at Delhi. I shall send them down to my agents in Calcutta for shipment to

England and I hope they will reach home all safe and that the girls will like the box and contents, although I fear they may not be as much approved of in England as they seem to be in this country. I had intended to send the pebbles home a long time ago but could never get them set to my satisfaction.

I have just been rather alarmed by a cry from the bungalow opposite to ours in which an officer of the regiment is living. We all ran out and found one of the servants' houses (close to the bungalow) in a blaze. The sepoys, on the alarm, turned out and pulled the thatch off in a minute and the water carriers being in readiness they and the men soon put a stop to it. The sepoys always behave well on these occasions, climbing on the roof without fear to pour water which others hand them from below in large earthen pots which are always at hand in case of fire. Had the fire reached the bungalow I fancy ours would have had a poor chance (with several others), as it is very near and a strong wind was blowing in the direction of it.

I have commenced the study of Punjabee again and am getting on pretty fairly. I shall try and pass the examinations while we are here although I have no interest with the Punjab administration (nor indeed with any other of the great Powers in India). I have already found the advantage of being ready for everything, in that way. As an instance I may tell you that I am at present acting interpreter for which I get some seventy rupees monthly, merely because I am the only passed officer with the corps. Punjabee is very easy and I hope to be able to master it before very long. My appointment as interpreter and quartermaster (for they always go together) gives me a good deal of work when combined with the adjutancy, but I suppose I shall not hold it long.

It is getting hot and we shall soon be shut up in our houses during the hot weather, I suppose. The Umballah people, such at least as can get leave, are daily leaving the plains for Simla, the nearest hill station. Most of the trades people are gone up there for the hot weather; in fact only those who are obliged to remain here do so as they have a delightful climate within sixty or seventy miles. I shall hope to run up for a month during the heat. I begin to think that six months in a cold climate would do me a great deal of good and set me up with a fresh stock of health and strength but I am afraid I cannot afford to lose my allowances for so long. I must try what a month will do I suppose. Do not think that I have anything to complain of in the way of health, although the fact is that after a continued residence in a hot climate everybody is the better for a few months of the cold and bracing air of the hills.

I have come to the end of my papers and, as I have not left time to read my letter through, I must even let it go as it is although doubtless full of mistakes and repetitions, as it had been written at various times and generally in a hurry. Hoping that this will find you all well and happy.

Believe me dear mother with kind love to all, ever your affectionate son, Robert H. Shebbeare

Ensign T.N. Walker, in memoirs written much later, gives an account of this march from Banda to Umballah, a distance of 436 miles.[4]

A long march in India in the cold season is most enjoyable. Dinner is soon after sunset, in order that the large mess-tent may be struck and started off with all the mess property before tattoo for the next camping-ground, where, on arrival next morning, it is found pitched and the table laid for breakfast.

This arrangement necessitates early to bed, which is just as well, for we have to turn out very early, the first bugle sounding from three to four o'clock in the morning, according to the length of the march before us. These marches vary from ten to fourteen miles ... Having 'fallen in', the regiment receives the order, 'Quick march', the band strikes up, and one feels in better humour. On the order to 'march at ease', pipes and cigars are lighted, and talking commences. Daylight appears; then the coffee-shop, which had been sent on with the mess property the night before, and left at a place as near half way to the new camping-ground as good and abundant drinking water was to be found.

There on the ground, as for a picnic, the Chottha haziri, or 'little breakfast', is laid out on a tablecloth, to which repast we all do ample justice. Half-an-hour is generally allowed for the halt, and on the corps marches again to the enlivening strains of the band ... Presently exclamations of 'There's the dueg buegy' are heard. This is a native kettle-drum which a camp-follower, sitting by the side of the road, beats at a distance of some six hundred yards from the new ground ... It gives notice to the villagers around that a regiment is coming, and thus an opportunity is afforded them of selling milk vegetables, fowls etc, etc, while the regiment learns that it is near the march's end ... Officers and men are generally white with dust. This, however, is soon got rid of, and, within half an hour the mess-tent is full of men tubbed, comfortably dressed, and pitching into a good breakfast.

Umballah, October 12th, 1855

My dear Joan,

I received your letter of the 30th August yesterday and I write at once in answer it; for my letter can just get home by the same steamer with the lady to whom I made over my little parcel. It has just occurred to me that I left blank the probable date of Mrs Sanctuary's arrival in England. I was not sure of it at the time I wrote and forgot (I think) to fill it in afterwards. If she does not send it shortly after you receive this tell Harry to go and find her out. I gave him the name and address. At any rate I hope he will call on her and know she will be glad to see him; and she may perhaps be able to tell him something more of our manner of life at Umballah than I have ever communicated in any of my letters. I only made her acquaintance since we came here but have been rather intimate with her since. I directed the parcel to Harry as I thought there might be some trouble about it and did not like to put my Father to the inconvenience which the looking after it might possibly occasion. I once thought of separating the articles and particularizing these intended for each of you, but I thought that I would leave it to my mother to do this for me, and I hope that trifling as the presents are you will all accept them with my most sincere love and will believe that I constantly think of you all and long to be with you, although I believe I am not much given to expressing this feeling in my letters.

As soon as ever I can see a chance of promotion within a year or two I shall give up my adjutancy and come home; but without this it would be folly to attempt it I think. I am now living very quietly and moderating my expenses with this hope before my eyes.

I, this day, received a letter from my friend Doyne from Calcutta telling me of his arrival and asking how he should send your parcel. I don't know when he may be here but suppose it will not be long first. I wish he had seen you and shall take him to task for not doing so but I believe he would have come if he could.

There will not be much change in Umballah this cold season as only one regiment marches. It is not very lively and I go out very little except to play cricket in the evening, or for a game at billiards occasionally. I am reading away at the Punjabee and I have gone once through both of the examination books. I shall try and go up for examination in January. I fear only the talking, as the test in this one is that one has to maintain a conversation with a man of the shopkeeper class, with one of the farming class and with a soldier, which will be difficult considering very few people speak the language at Umballah and I have therefore very little practice. The examinations take place at Lahore and I shall require about ten days leave to go there. I fear I shall get little good at passing but I can get no harm. I am at present holding only the adjutancy[5] but in a few days shall be interpreter and possibly quartermaster as I am the only passed officer present and I think they will scarcely let an unpassed man hold the appointment.

I am writing my letter and reading at intervals the Quarterly Review of the 'Memoirs of Sydney Smith'. I should like much to see the book although I think, by reading this review and another which appeared a short time back (I forget where), I have probably got the best part of it already. 28th. I must finish off in a hurry to save the mail. I don't recollect a bit what I have told you but I have at any rate written something and will write again soon.

Your ever affectionate brother, Robert H. Shebbeare

Notes

1 Extract from J.P. Riddell's 'Record of the 60th Regiment of Bengal Native Infantry: With a Sequel on the 3rd Europeans', *Journal of the Society for Army Historical Research* (War Office), 1964.

2 This was Brevet Major (acting Lieutenant Colonel) Richard Drought. Robert Shebbeare does not mince his words about his opinion of him, and mentions his acting CO in similarly derogatory tones in a later letter (7 June 1857). Drought joined the Regiment at Agra in 1825, was present at the siege and capture of Bhurtpore in 1825–6, and saw active service with the 60th on several occasions. He served in Major General Pollock's force that recaptured Kabul in 1842. Later he was wounded at Delhi (see comments from RHS in later letter about this!). He retired in 1861 as an Honorary Major General. As his adjutant, Robert Shebbeare must have had a lot to do with Drought, so one must assume that this opinion was not lightly formed, especially as he is very complimentary about Colonel Seaton, who replaced Drought. At the time of the Mutiny, Drought would have been aged fifty-five.

3 Hodson, a friend of Robert Shebbeare, and not noted for reticence on any subject, said:

> At the age at which officers become colonels and majors, not one in fifty is able to stand the wear and tear of Indian service. They become still more worn in mind than in body. All elasticity is gone; all energy and enterprise worn out; they become, after a fortnight's campaign, a burden to themselves, an annoyance to those under them, and a terror to everyone but the enemy!
>
> The officer who commanded the cavalry brigade which so disgraced the service at Chillianwalla, was not able to mount a horse without the assistance of two men. A brigadier of infantry, under whom I served during the three most critical days of the late war, could not see his regiment when I led his horse by the bridle until its nose touched the bayonets; and even then he said faintly, 'Pray which way are the men facing, Mr. Hodson?'

In the emergency, a large number of them were replaced by younger men and very often lieutenants were asked to raise regiments, as was Robert Shebbeare in 1858. One aspect of the rigid system that seems to have been more flexible is that officers were moved between regiments quite frequently.

4 Walker, Colonel T.N., *Through the Mutiny: Reminiscences of Thirty Years Active Service and Sport in India, 1854–66*, Gibbings and Co., London, 1907.

5 From 1 October 1855 to September 1856, as Adjutant of the 60th NI, he kept a memo book in which he recorded details of promotion and pay of officers and sepoys, together with the general business in which the regiment was involved. A page from December 1855 gives some typical entries:

> Ramchurn Gowall, Sepoy, No. 7 company, absent without leave from 6th December. Struck off R.O., [regimental orders] 26th December, 1855.
>
> Naick [corporal] Bhowanycheek Duobee put in arrest on the 23rd December.
>
> Captain Coare, Lt Innes and Ensign Walker and companies 2, 3 and 4, completed to full strength, to be held in readiness to proceed to Kalka for protection at Hd. Qtrs. Camp. Brigade Orders 24th December, 1855.

Naick Bhola Sing died at Delhi. Struck off R.O., 26th December 1855.

Complaint of Lolemun Bunniah against 7 drummers.

To send receipt for 4/2 Rupees hire of 2 carts from Kurnaul with sick.

60 men from above 3 companies – marched on afternoon of 26th December to escort treasure to Kalka.

5 recruits entered R.O. 27th December.

Chapter Two

MUTINY

There were a number of reasons why the Indian Mutiny happened
and opinions differ as to which of many factors was the most
important. It is generally agreed, however, that the explosion
of violence which occurred was the culmination of many years of
simmering resentment about a number of issues, not only in the
ranks of the army but in the country at large.

When the annexation of the Indian states began, it was thought
that the administration would work best if run along lines which
took account of the customs and practices of a particular locality
but, as the bureaucracy grew, a system evolved which devalued
the contribution of the native civil servants and left Europeans
with salaries and career prospects that were far superior, which
naturally caused resentment. Educated Indians began to realize
that their religious, social and cultural customs were in great
danger of being sidelined in favour of the Western sets of values
which were being superimposed on their traditional ways. Writing
in 1858, Syed Ahmad Khan stated that the main cause of rebellion
had been the lack of understanding of Indian ways, which stemmed
from the exclusion of any native representation on the Legislative
Council of India.

The annexation in 1856 of Oude, one of the largest and richest
provinces in northern India, from which a very large number
of sepoys of the Bengal army were recruited, caused deep resentment. Not only was their king, despite his many faults, removed,
and their land put under direct British rule, but the taxation
system was changed in such a way that it alienated several of the

most powerful feudal landowners, who became rebel leaders the following year.

Within the army itself many grievances had built up over the years, of which the issue of caste was but one. The British had traditionally recruited high-caste Hindus of the warrior class because they were tall, imposing men who made good soldiers, but in 1834 the recruiting base was widened to include Sikhs, Muslims and Hindus of lower caste, a dilution which was not welcomed. The regiments raised in Oude, in particular, were outraged by the recruitment of Punjabis and Sikhs. Batta, an allowance for foreign service, was withdrawn in 1849, and in 1856, very controversially, an order was made that all new enlistment was to be for General Service rather than for service within India, which meant that Hindus might have to travel across seas, thereby defiling their caste.

Regular pay, a pension and the chance of plunder as a perk of the job were the main incentives for the rank and file to join what was basically a mercenary army run by officers of an alien race and religion, but over the years there had been an erosion of some of these. During the early part of the nineteenth century there had been a number of campaigns that had given sepoys opportunity for booty, but as this source of revenue diminished they were left, not only with a life of boring routine, but with a wage of seven rupees a month that had not changed since the beginning of the century. Grain prices had risen steadily during the same period and they had to provide their own food by buying produce from the local population, so in real terms the standard of living was obviously diminishing. From this wage they also had to find deductions for certain items of dress and equipment, which they disliked wearing because of the tight-fitting discomfort quite unsuited to the Indian climate, and they had to pay for the transport of their baggage when moving from station to station. When in cantonments, the men were responsible for building their own huts, and conditions were generally very squalid.

Native officers, all of whom were subordinate to the most junior of British officers, were particularly frustrated in a number of ways. There was a ceiling on the rank that they could attain, and promotion, based on length of service, was extremely slow. For ambitious and talented men this lack of career opportunity was, as much as anything, responsible for enabling them to see the

21

solution that a rebellion might offer, and was the reason why so many officers took a leading part in it. In addition, the attitude of many British officers to native soldiers had undergone a change for the worse over the years, and there was amongst some of the latter the justified feeling that they were treated very much as inferiors.

So, with much of the country feeling threatened by foreign domination, and with particular disgruntlement within the army, the stage was set for trouble and in early 1857 a catalyst was added to the already explosive mix.

Since 1840, the Company armies had been using percussion muskets with a smooth bore and although rifles had been in limited use, for a long time they had had technical problems, so that it was not until 1856 that the first batch of the 1853 Enfield rifles reached India. This was still a muzzle-loading weapon that depended on the soldier biting the top off a cartridge, pouring the powder followed by the rest of the cartridge down the barrel, and then ramming down the bullet or ball. To make it sufficiently easy for the new Enfield cartridge to be rammed down the rifled bore, it needed to be greased. The C-in-C of the Bengal Army had warned in 1853 that whatever was used for the purpose should not be offensive to the native soldiers, but this advice was ignored and by 1856 the ordnance department started to make its own cartridges to a recipe containing tallow, but not specifying of which kind it should be. Before any of them could even be issued, rumours began to circulate that the grease was made from cow and pig fat, offensive to both Hindu and Muslim. The army, to its credit, took a number of steps to try to remedy the situation, but by now the seditionists had seized on this opportunity to ferment a general rising and nothing that was said or done made much difference. Organized cells of rebel sepoys spread rumours that the greased cartridges were being used in a deliberate attempt on the part of the British government to undermine their religion and caste, and to force them to adopt Christianity. Trouble flared up in February when sepoys of the 19th Bengal Native Infantry refused to take up the cartridges. At Ambala in March, where Robert Shebbeare was stationed with the 60th BNI, there was a musketry depot to which sepoys from numerous regiments came to be instructed in the use of the new Enfield rifle, and here the concerns reached such a pitch that General Anson, C-in-C India, had to postpone the use of the cartridges for live firing.

Early in the year the mysterious business of the chapatties also occurred, when a single biscuit was brought to the watchman of a village with instructions to bake four more and distribute these to other villages. Thus, in a short time, they had appeared over an enormous area and created a great deal of speculation about their significance. Amongst the people at the time, some thought it was part of the government plot to convert them to another religion; others thought it was a token to warn them to be ready for some unspecified impending catastrophe. Some of the British thought that it had a connection to an event in Madras a hundred years before, when cakes had been spread around prior to mutiny; others maintained that it might be linked to the Hindu prophecy, shared also by Muslims, that British rule would only last for a century. At all events, the rumours surrounding the chapatties had the desired effect of unsettling both the British and the Indians.

On 29 March, Mungul Pandy, a Brahmin of the 34th BNI, high on drugs, attacked his adjutant and sergeant major and made an unsuccessful attempt to rouse the rest of the regiment to mutiny. He and another man of the same name were both hanged on the parade ground at Barrackpore in April, giving rise to the nickname of 'Pandies' being then applied to all the rebel troops.

The events which finally lit the touch paper occurred in the large garrison at Meerut in April and early May, where there was an unusually high proportion of European troops. Here, eighty-five skirmishers of the 3rd Light Cavalry, one of the oldest and most highly respected native regiments in India, refused to accept an order by their heavy handed and unpopular CO to use the new cartridges, on the grounds that they would be ostracized by all in the army if they did so. All were court-martialled and sentenced to ten years in prison with hard labour; on 9 May they were shackled on the parade ground, in front of their fellows, and sent off to the civilian gaol. Despite being warned that there were plans afoot for the Indian troops to rise up and release them, the Colonel and the station commander, Brigadier Archdale Wilson, took no action. On Sunday, 10 May, the 11th and 20th BNI, together with the 3rd Cavalry, rose up in force, killing almost fifty British officers, together with their wives and children. Indecision by the British commanders allowed the mutineers to escape and, although

23

most of them were keen to go home, they were persuaded by the rebel leaders to set off for Delhi where, the next day, sowars (troopers) from the 3rd Cavalry set the overthrow of the city in motion.

The day chosen by the rebel leaders as the one on which all the native regiments of the Bengal Army would rise up and overwhelm the British soldiers was 10 May 1857. This day, being a Sunday, had been chosen in the expectation that the mutineers would catch the soldiers and their families in church without arms, ammunition and horses, and would be able to massacre them as they came out. The month of May had been chosen because, being in the hottest part of the year, the conspirators thought that any survivors who managed to escape would die of sunstroke and exposure to the searing heat. Fortunately, the events which took place at Meerut, where many of the Europeans were massacred, were not repeated everywhere else as the men of many other regiments held back to see what might be happening, and as a result the mutinies occurred in a sporadic fashion, giving the British time to consolidate a response.

In his recent book, *The Indian Mutiny, 1857*, Saul David has made a masterly and very readable survey of the evidence available to date, and gives a detailed analysis of the many intertwined events that took place.

Umballah, May 18th, 1857

My dear father,

As you will probably hear disastrous news from this part of the country I just scribble a line as we have this moment heard that communication is open from Bombay.

We are all quiet at Umballah and the sepoys still faithful although very much excited. We expect all to march for Delhi in a few days and I hope our advance will check the whole business.

We can hear nothing from down country but the Punjab is reported quiet.

You shall have a letter by every possible opportunity but I fancy there is a poor chance of this letter even.

I am very hard worked as we all are and I don't get much sleep but as I was beginning to get slightly corpulent I have no fear that the work will injure me – it will rather have a contrary effect.

I have no time to add to this note as the mail is just going out – I heard the chance only just now.

With kindest love to dear mother and all at home,
believe me ever your affectionate son,
Robert Shebbeare

Camp Mundlana, which you will not find on the map, I fancy, 30th May, 1857

My dear Harry,

Scorching weather! No thermometer in camp but I should suppose 120 degrees in the tent to be about the mark. I wrote to my father before we started and hope he would get the letter and set your minds at ease, as the most wonderfully exaggerated reports will of course reach you as to the fate of the north western provinces.

I had better give you a slight sketch of our proceedings of late. On the 22nd we got (about sunset) our orders to march at midnight. We went down to Kurnaul by the regular marches and halted one day. We were then told that the Treasury at Rohtuck some sixty miles SW was in danger and were ordered to march by double marches for its protection, but when we arrived at Paneeputt where the advanced guard of the army was, we heard that 600 mutineers from Delhi had gone out and robbed the Treasury and got safe back.

We found Mr Lock the Collector of Rohtuck at Paneeputt whither he had escaped on horseback after seeing his house set fire to. We marched off next morning with him and made a second march today to a village in his district, the name of which is at the top of my note. We hear all sorts of terrible reports of atrocities committed in Rohtuck by the rebels but I believe nothing that I do not see unless on the authority of European eyewitnesses. Poor Lock's property however was utterly destroyed without doubt, to the extent of some 10,000 Rupees. Our arrival in the district sets matters to rights wherever we are seen but we shall have to burn some villages and shoot or hang some of the head men of them before all is quiet. The forces are concentrating on Delhi and I fancy you will probably get a good account of it before you receive this scribble, which I only send you to assure you of my own safety. I am keeping a horseman waiting while I write this so I cannot extend it. I am trying to get the authorities here to raise a party of irregular horse and shall try and get command of it if they will do so – but I don't know how things will turn out. Our sepoys are behaving very well.

I will write on every possible occasion – assure my father and mother and all at home of my constant love

and believe me dear Harry,

ever your affectionate Robert H. Shebbeare

Rohtuck, June 7th, 1857

My dear mother,

I have written two letters since I left Umballah. The first would no doubt reach you, the second I doubt about and therefore send off another on the chance of its going, although the road is in such a state that there is no certainty. We had no letters for four days, until yesterday we received one from headquarters.

Our sepoys are behaving very well indeed and I really hope that all will go well with the regiment. Immediately on the outbreak the Commander-in-Chief removed a Colonel from another regiment to command the 60th which was a very great relief to us all for Colonel Drought, besides being a very disagreeable commanding officer, was utterly unfit for the emergency. Colonel Seaton who now commands us is a good soldier and a gentleman on whom it is a pleasure to serve. This Rohtuck is a horrible place, sandy and hot to the last degree. We have no shade for our tents but have been able to make up a rough sort of tattie of the camel thorn plant, and by keeping them constantly wet we manage to pass the day without injury from the heat. We are now getting short of supplies, but I hope we shall be able to get a cart from Umballah before long. In three or four days we shall have no beer or wine in camp and the prospect is not pleasant as the water is inclined to be salt. We are hourly expecting news that a decisive blow has been struck at Delhi – some of us thought we heard guns fired last night but we were probably deceived as the distance (some forty to forty-five miles) is very great and I think the sound would scarcely reach us. We have had a good deal of sickness in camp but I am glad to say no officer has been attacked as yet. There is no money in camp, nor is it likely that we shall get any just now, as the villagers make great difficulties about paying their revenue – they are evidently waiting to see what is done at Delhi.

My house is now left to take care of itself, I fancy, as I heard the guard has been removed to help garrison the churchyard where all the inhabitants have collected their property. As we get no news, I must confine myself to news regarding myself, and I think I have told you all. I have not received letters from England for some time, but I suppose I shall get the missing letters when the road is open again.

With kindest regards

ever your affectionate son

Robert H. Shebbeare

Part of letter postmarked Umballah, 13th May:

I send by Marseilles that you may get the letter earlier. European troops at Umballah 9th Lancers 75th Foot 1st Bengal European Fusiliers 2nd Bengal European Fusiliers two Troops European Horse Artillery.

Camp before Delhi, 11th July, 1857

My dearest mother,

I have written you several letters of late since the disturbances commenced but the post is so very uncertain that I cannot calculate for certain on your receiving them and will therefore recapitulate to a certain extent.

About the end of May we were ordered to march with a force towards Delhi. On reaching Paneeputt twenty miles from Kurnaul we were sent off to keep the peace at Rohtuck. We remained there until the 9th June, when our Regiment mutinied and the Grenadier Company fired on us. About four p.m. we were almost all asleep or engaged in writing in the mess tent, when we heard a discharge of muskets and some sepoys rushed up and told us that the Grenadier Company were under arms and that they had told our grooms to get our horses ready that we might escape, as it would be impossible for us to remain in camp. The Colonel (Seaton) went down to the lines and I followed him immediately, but the Grenadiers began to fire on us and the men of the other companies turned us back and begged us to escape. My horse had been saddled and I jumped on and was about to start when I saw that Col. Seaton was not ready, so I had to stay for him under a pretty smart fire. However, we got safely away and after hanging about the neighbourhood of the camp for about two hours, we started for Delhi (about forty-five miles); we had one man on foot with us and had therefore to travel at a foot pace. We started at about 7.30 pm and reached the camp at Delhi at about 7.30 the next day after a most fatiguing ride, as the weather was very hot. Thank God, we arrived without any officer being badly wounded. The villagers were very civil as they thought the Regiment was behind us – not having heard of the mutiny. My different friends in camp were very kind and furnished me with a suit of clothes. I had escaped in my shirtsleeves, as had most of us.

(The second part of this letter concerns events in Delhi, so it has been moved to the beginning of the next chapter.)

Robert Shebbeare's account of the mutiny of the 60th BNI in May and June 1857 is fairly sparse in its detail, which is quite understandable given that, as Adjutant of a regiment of 900 men, he was kept extremely busy all the time and, in addition, it all took place during the searing heat of the Indian hot season.

Two other accounts by officers of the Regiment, both written at leisure long after the events in Umballah and Rohtuck, give colour and substance to some of the laconic observations that Robert Shebbeare made in his letters home. In the light of these later accounts, which describe graphically the extreme danger that the officers of the 60th were in at the time, it seems probable that Robert Shebbeare's economy of detail was prompted not only by lack of time, but by a desire to spare his family too much alarm regarding his safety, as he would have been aware that vivid newspaper reports of atrocities and casualties were being published in the English newspapers.

The narrative which follows is drawn from the reminiscences of both Lieutenant Walker,[1] acting Captain, and Colonel Seaton,[2] Commanding Officer of the 60th from 15 May, and will serve to give some idea of the circumstances in which the English officers found themselves, well as giving the reader an account of the role that Robert Shebbeare played in it all. (Their contributions have been marked 'W' and 'S' at the end of each excerpt.)

On Sunday, May 10th, my regiment the 60th B.N.I. mutinied, and broke into the bells of arms. Each company had one to itself, in which the sepoys deposited, after each parade and duty, their muskets, bayonets, belts, and pouches, which contained twenty or thirty rounds of ammunition. These were kept under lock and key.

My pay-havildar, or sergeant, appeared breathlessly at my bungalow at about 10 am, and reported to me that the sepoys had mutinied, and were breaking open the bells of arms. The old gentleman begged me to ride down at once to the lines. I mounted my horse and galloped down, making at once for the centre bell of arms of the five contained in the block belonging to the right wing of the regiment, for it belonged to No. 2 Company, of which I was in charge, as the captain was on furlough in England.

I at once saw that I was only just in time, for the Grenadiers and No. 3 Company had broken into theirs, were putting on their belts, and had their muskets in their hands. I pushed through the crowd of men and turned a number of sepoys of No. 2 Company away from the door of their bell of arms.

28

If fierce looks could have killed me I should have been a dead man, perhaps I should say boy, on the spot. The door of No. 2 Company was inside a portico which the others had not. This served as a sentry-box for the sentry, who was always posted over the block of five.

I thrust myself into this, and putting my back against the door, defended it. I implored the men not to disgrace the company as others had done theirs. I heard the door of No. 1 Company burst open and the men shout.

Men of the Grenadiers and other companies with fixed bayonets came up and yelled insolently to me 'to come out'. Others were loading their muskets, and one man said, 'All right, I will shoot you there.' I told him that if he did he would blow the whole place up, for the ammunition inside would explode. Luckily for me he believed it, and with an oath came down to the 'ready'.

One man lowered his bayonet and said to me, 'Come out or I will bayonet you.' The sentry, quite a young lad, stood in front of the portico, apparently quite stupefied. I ordered him to come down to the charge position and help me defend the door. He instantly obeyed, and as quickly was knocked over, disarmed, and disappeared.

The man, with his bayonet lowered, approached nearer to me, threatening as before. I was making up my mind to spring at him and possess myself of his musket and bayonet, when the old pay-sergeant appeared on the scene. He forced himself to me, and, knocking the bayonet down, said, 'I am a Brahmin, and you will first have to kill me, then the lieutenant, and then you will get this door open.' Killing a Brahmin, or man of the priest caste, is looked upon as sacrilege by Hindus. The old gentleman put himself in front of me. The loaded muskets were lowered, and the sergeant said to me, 'Do not you argue with them, sahib; let me.' A tall dark-complexioned sepoy, with whom I had often practised wrestling and single-stick in the regimental sports shed, with his bayonet fixed and musket at the trail, caught hold of the pay-sergeant's arm and tried to pull him out of the portico, saying, 'I am a Brahmin too, come out of this.' I seized the musket and bayonet out of the man's hand, and we pushed him out. I shall never forget the man's face as he abused me. He rushed up to another sepoy and seized his loaded musket. The pay-sergeant, calling the man by his name (he was a Tewarrie, but the other name I forget), asked him, 'What are you going to do?' Other sepoys shouted at him and I heard the word 'Magazine'. It was evident that they feared an explosion if the man fired at me.

29

At this moment Colonel Drought appeared on the scene. He called out, 'What is all this about, my children?' The men congregated around him; the dark man went too. The good old pay-sergeant said to me, 'Buch gea, sahib!' (We have escaped, sir).

The colonel, on seeing me, called me up to him. The sergeant said, 'Go, sir; I will guard the door.' I gave him the musket and bayonet and went to the colonel, the sepoys making way for me.

They were pointing to a troop of Horse Artillery, manned by Englishmen, and complaining that they were turned out to fire on the regiment, giving this as the reason for their behaviour. It was just the other way; the troop turned out in consequence of their mutinying.

The colonel asked me if I had got my horse, and on my answering in the affirmative, he ordered me to ride up to the officer commanding the troop and to beg of him not to bring his guns down, as the men dreaded their appearance on parade, and he feared it would drive them to mutiny!

After delivering this message, I told the officer the actual mutinous state of things. He then withdrew his troop behind a barrack out of sight of our men. I galloped back to the colonel, and, on my reaching him the sepoys shouted out, 'Bravo, Walker, Sahib!' And these were the villains who a few minutes before were abusing me and threatening my life!

Other officers of the regiment had appeared on the scene, and the men commenced to return their arms and accoutrement. So ended the awful May 10, 1857, so far as my regiment was concerned. (W)

On 11 May, the 5th NI, whose lines were next to the 60th, mutinied and seized their arms, but later returned them.

The next day, General Sir Henry Barnard ordered the regiment to parade, and addressed the men. He told them that he had heard of all that had occurred, and as he felt sure that it arose from groundless excitement on the men's part, he would overlook it, but ordered the two colours to be brought forward and the Regiment to pass by them in single file, each man to kiss both colours, to show loyalty and fidelity. The officers were afterwards told by spectators that after kissing the colours and going a short way past them, each sepoy spat on the ground, which amongst Asiatics means contempt and scorn. 'After this, to show the great confidence the British officers placed in their men, we were ordered to sleep at night on the roads between the huts ... my confidence in the sepoy kept my hand on my Tranter's revolver.' (W)

30

Colonel Seaton arrived in Umballah to take command on 15 May and was at once bearded by a gentleman who said he had just seen a sepoy loading a musket close by.

I got my glass, and on looking at the sepoy found that he was one of the 60th NI, the very 'babes' I had come to command. Without a moment's delay I put on my sword, jumped into the buggy, and drove off to the quarters of the adjutant, the gallant and lamented Lieutenant Shebbeare.

I immediately told him my errand, and we went at once to the commanding officer [Drought], to whom I produced my credentials, and then assumed the command. In five minutes I was on the way to the men's lines, and as we went along I explained to Lieutenant Shebbeare the incident that had occurred at the Travellers' Bungalow.

The relieved guards were immediately paraded, and I inspected each musket separately. Of course not one was found loaded, nor was I particularly anxious at the moment to make the discovery. Had any preconcerted plan for a rising existed, we should have found many muskets loaded, or the men would have committed some act that would have betrayed their purpose. The state of the regiment was well known. There was a large force of Europeans in the cantonment. The native regiments were therefore powerless, if, as we hoped, proper measures were taken with them.

I told the men my reason for inspecting their arms, I also said that I was glad to find that the sepoys had been calumniated; and that I hoped to learn that much of what I had heard of them was misrepresented.

As I could not find any house near enough to the regiment, Lieutenant Shebbeare kindly placed a couple of rooms in his bungalow at my disposal. Living under the same roof with the adjutant was most convenient, for it enabled me to acquire in a very short time all the information that was necessary regarding the regiment, to which, of course, I was a perfect stranger. (S)

On the same day, 15 May, the Commander-in-Chief, General the Hon. George Anson, arrived at Umballah for the purpose of leading the field force that he was assembling in great haste for the purpose of advancing on Delhi. On the 16th he held a council of war and the question of disarming the 60th and 5th NI was considered. That he himself had grave doubts about them is shown by his comment: 'They are still doing their duties and will be retained as part of this force, but it is impossible to conceal from

31

oneself that there is some hazard in employing them on this service. The conduct of the Native Army has destroyed all confidence in any regiment, notwithstanding that they may still profess to be faithful and loyal.'[3]

Seaton records:

I was astonished that there should be the smallest doubt on the subject; but it appeared that, when the regiment had shown strong symptoms of disaffection, by standing to its arms on the 10th, as part of some preconcerted plan, and had been quieted by Sir H. Barnard, some sort of promise had been made or implied, that they should not be disarmed.

No English officer likes to retire from a promise once given or implied; hence the honourable scruple to adopt what had now become a necessary measure of self-preservation. I strongly advocated the disarming, and was so far successful that I left the council table with the order in my pocket to disarm the regiment at four o'clock that afternoon.

A few minutes before that time I told this to the adjutant [Shebbeare] as we were going to the parade ordered but on arriving at the ground, I found the Persian interpreter to the commander-in-chief, accompanied by the military secretary and aide-de-camp, there before me. The Chief, it appeared had changed his mind, and the Persian interpreter addressed the regiment, assuring them that they would go with the force to Delhi, and have an opportunity of showing their faithfulness and retrieving their character. I was indignant and disgusted, for I knew full well what would come of it, and foretold it at the council table; but as I was bound to make the best of it I addressed the men, who one and all swore fidelity to their colours and the Sircar [government]. It was, in the main a useless ceremony, but it quieted the minds of the officers, sobered the sepoys a little, and kept them quiet for a short time. The two native regiments were close together on the extreme left of the cantonment, the officers' bungalows just behind the lines, and had the men broken out into open revolt, as at Meerut, we might have been murdered, one and all, long before help could have reached us. The sepoys, indeed, were in such a state that a trifle might have roused the demon within them. Under the circumstances, it seemed politic to seem to trust them. (S)

On 22 May, the 75th Queen's Regiment plus the 1st and 2nd European Bengal Fusiliers also arrived at Umballah to join the 9th Lancers and European Horse Artillery.

32

These formed the nucleus of what later became called the 'Delhi Field Force', which soon set off for Delhi. The 60th also marched with them but there was so much distrust and disgust that when they arrived at Paneeput the Regiment was ordered to march on to Rohtuck, on the pretext that they were to collect revenue, but in reality to free the force of a dangerous element (see Note 1).

Seaton's version of the reason for being sent to Rohtuck differs here (and one must assume that his, as CO, was the right one) for he says that on 25 May, Colonel Chester, the Adjutant-General, gave him orders from the C-in-C to march to Rohtuck to intercept the Hurrianah Light Infantry, who, with the 4th Irregular Cavalry, had mutinied at Hansi and Hissar.

Yet the regiment [the 60th], which had not only mutinied, but had long been looked on as composed of a turbulent, ill-conducted set of men, was deliberately sent to within a short distance of the very centre and focus of rebellion – to a place most convenient in the world for their purpose, and far from the control of English troops, on the pretence of intercepting two regiments that had just mutinied, and had massacred not only the English officers, but their wives and children, with atrocities equal to those committed at Meerut.

Rohtuck is just forty-five miles from Delhi; there is a fine metalled road the whole way connecting the two places, and there was nothing on earth to prevent the men murdering us all, and joining the mutineers with their arms, camp-equipment, and a full complement of service ammunition.

I had known Colonel Chester for years, but so thoroughly was he ashamed of the order, that when he communicated it he did not lift his eyes from the paper before him. It was a cruel, half-hearted measure, loudly condemned by every one in the force in stronger language than I should like to commit to paper, for not a soul ever expected to see me or my officers again.

However, orders must be obeyed; no officer can flinch from them, even if he knows he is going to certain death. So I put a good face on the matter, spoke kindly to the men and cheerily to the officers, who, I must do them the justice to say, behaved manfully through this terrible trial.

What had now come to pass I had foretold at the council of war. The European soldiers, who had heard of the mutiny, and of the atrocities perpetrated at Meerut, and had witnessed the conduct of the 60th at Umballa, were now so suspicious of them that they loudly declared they would not have that regiment in camp [at Paneeput]. The Commander-in-Chief saw his mistake when too late, and the only plan he and his staff could think of was to send the 60th to Rohtuck, consigning me and my officers, as every one believed, to certain death. (S)

The night before we left Paneeput, we British officers were entertained at dinner by the officers of the 1st European Fusiliers, who thought, as we did ourselves, that we were going to certain death, and when our healths were drunk we were assured that they would erect a monument to our memories. A number of us had been at the Honourable East India Company's military college, Addiscombe, at the same time as many of them, and some of the young officers quite recently, and although we knew very well that our chances of ever again seeing other white faces than our own were slight, it did not spoil our dinners, or the fun of the evening.

With regret and disappointment at the idea of not joining, as we thought, in the attack on Delhi, we marched out of Paneeput at an early hour the following morning for Rohtuck, a town some fifty or sixty miles east of Paneeput. As we marched through the city the British officers were treated with jeers, and in several instances with stones or brickbats. A new commanding officer, Colonel T. Seaton, afterwards Sir Thomas Seaton, K.C.B., had joined us just before we left Umballah.

On the 27th May, the regiment halted at a grove of mango-trees, and a young sepoy of the Grenadiers deliberately tried to inflame one of his officers with his insubordinate behaviour, and Seaton had to intervene before the situation got out of hand. He called him up before him, and, instead of punishing him, he gave him a lecture, and said that as he was generally a well-behaved man, he forgave him. The man, who had been expecting at least to be court-marshalled, was quite taken aback and subdued, and a dangerous situation averted. (W)

On the next march some of the camp followers were murdered by the local inhabitants in quest of plunder.

The heat was now terrible. The country, a succession of undulating sandy ridges and mounds, was covered with a low prickly bush, and except along the banks of the canal, where there were a few fields still green, there was not the slightest appearance of verdure. As we approached Rohtuck, which is not far from the Bickaneer country, the country assumed a very desolate appearance ... and the hot wind as we marched along blew with fury.

Our only plan to keep ourselves cool in camp was to pile up loosely in the doorways of our tents on the windward side, the little prickly bushes before mentioned. When these were well sprinkled with water, the wind rushing through them was cooled by evaporation, and the atmosphere of the tent was rendered bearable.

The day we reached Rohtuck I made a long march of eighteen miles, being anxious to get there to meet the Hurrianah Light Infantry. I intended to address the 60th, point to the men as cowards who had debased their name and sex by the murder of helpless women and children, and then try to bring them into collision before any communication could pass between them. It was our only hope to save the regiment; and if, whilst I was addressing the men, or we were preparing to attack the mutineers, the 60th should show signs of turning against us, being armed and mounted, and our horses at hand, we should stand a better chance of escape than if the regiment were to break into revolt at night, or attack us when unarmed and unprepared. I marched at 11 pm, at which hour there was a hot parching sand blowing in our faces, bringing from the Bickaneer Desert clouds of light sand and dust that filled our eyes and choked our nostrils. Let my readers fancy a strong March wind with the heat of the fiercest day in July they can remember, and they will have a faint resemblance of that through which we painfully toiled. The march was most painful to all of us; we had not slept at all during the day, nor much during the preceding night, and as the wind abated a little towards one o'clock, sleep tried to creep over our eyes. I was obliged to dismount from my horse and walk; to keep my eyes open; but as I moved along I fell asleep, and was wakened by a stumble that nearly brought me to the ground, an incident which happened several times. (S)

On another day's march, one of the sepoys, a recruit, dropped his lotah, a brass drinking vessel, down a well when drawing water. On the bugle sounding the 'fall-in', the men refused to do so, giving as their excuse that the man could not go without his lotah. Colonel Seaton, who could read their thoughts, as it were, went up to the well, and asked the lad how much the lotah had cost him. On his replying 'four rupees', the colonel took that sum out of his pocket and, handing it over, said, 'Here, buy another one, and let the villagers have your old one.' The lad smiled and pocketed the money. Then the colonel, turning towards the men, said, 'Now that is settled, fall in.' The whole regiment did so at once. They were foiled in getting an excuse for another mutiny. If the usual method of enforcing discipline had been attempted, the well would probably have been our [the officers'] tomb.' (W)

It is interesting to see how Seaton's own much fuller account of this incident differs in detail, if not in essence, from Walker's:

Outside the village was a large well, shaded by a few trees, round which the men eagerly clustered to draw water and satisfy their craving thirst. As soon as all needful precautions were taken, I got some refreshment myself, and then lay down by the road-side on my horse-cloth, my officers around me. When the allotted hour had expired, I desired the adjutant [Shebbeare] to have the usual call sounded for the men to fall in. The officers at once repaired to their several posts, but the soldiers came slowly, and with apparent reluctance, many of them still lingering round the well and talking loudly to each other. I had the call repeated, and then went to the well myself to hurry the men off. I was not at all surprised at their delay, for, as there was but this one well for the whole regiment, and as the men wore their woollen coats and had a good weight to carry, the heat and dust must have made them awfully thirsty, and many would draw water twice, or even three times.

When I came near enough to be heard, I called out — 'Now, men, don't delay; fall in quickly, and let us get this march over in the cool of the morning.' These words were followed by perfect silence, while one of the men came up, and saluting with his musket at the old 'Recover', said, in an abrupt and rather rough way –

'My lotah has fallen into the well: I want leave to stay behind to get it out.'

I had reason to suspect that this was a mere excuse to remain behind for some purpose; but, instead of refusing leave, something prompted me to say quietly (all paying great attention) –

'What is the value of your lotah?'

'A rupee and a half, sahib.'

'Did you hear yesterday that the people of this country killed some of our camp followers ?'

'Yes, Colonel Sahib.'

'Well, don't be so foolish as to stay behind and risk your life for this trifle. Come on into camp, and I will give you a new one. A lotah is nothing to me, but a sepoy's life is a great deal.'

The man's demeanour changed. After making due acknowledgements, he snapped his fingers, and called out, cheerily, 'Come along, brothers, you hear what the Colonel Sahib says — fall in quickly.'

36

In five minutes we were off. My reflections at the moment were that a few kind words and a little sympathy will have their effect even on these disaffected men; and I thought no more of the matter. (S)

Later, on reaching Delhi, a Sikh servant told him that the whole business had been stage-managed by the men of the Grenadier Company, and that had he been high-handed with the sepoy with the 'lost' lotah he would have been shot by him, as his musket was loaded.

While on the march to Rohtuck we struck on a road on which a mutinied regiment, The Hurrianah Light Infantry, had just marched en route for Delhi. So eager were they to get out of the way, luckily for us, that they left a quantity of their baggage at the crossroads. Our colonel halted us, and explained to the men that as this was the property of murderers and mutineers they might help themselves to it. Not a thing was touched, which we looked upon as a bad sign. (W)

Again, Seaton's account differs slightly in detail.

We reached Rohtuck at sunrise, and found that the Hurrianah Light Infantry had passed through the day before, marching rapidly on Delhi. They had not only abandoned some carts and baggage, but had also left behind some women – circumstances which showed they were in desperate haste. Several dead bodies lay extended on the road, apparently sepoys; but I could gain no reliable information regarding them, excepting they were not natives of Rohtuck. The people of the town said that there had been a dispute about division of plunder, which was not at all unlikely. (S)

There is no mention of the offer to the men to help themselves to the baggage!

The regiment camped in the grounds of the government offices, which had been ransacked and burnt by the rebels, and for three days, apart from enduring the heat and discomfort, little of note occurred.

On 4 June another incident took place, about which Seaton and Walker's accounts are at some variance, but one might incline towards the Colonel's recollection as being the more reliable.

On the 4th June I was in the mess-tent writing to the adjutant-general, to whom I was reporting the hopeless state of the regiment, which I said it would be impossible to keep together unless I could get information that Delhi was taken, or that we had been successful in some engagement against the rebels, when the adjutant came in and said, 'Colonel, I wish particularly to speak to you.'

It was close on 5 pm; and as several officers were in the tent, I went outside with the adjutant.

'Well, Shebbeare, what is it?'

'Why, Colonel, I have just heard from two of our drummers, who have their information from particular friends amongst the men, that the regiment is to mutiny tonight, murder the officers, and be off to Delhi.' (I quote his words exactly)

Although I had it constantly in mind that this catastrophe would surely overtake us, it was startling enough to hear it was so close at hand. And now that the difficulty stared me in the face, how, with this small body of officers, in the midst of a wild country, and surrounded by an inimical population, was I to meet and grapple with reckless and determined mutineers? It was not to be put off or evaded, had we wished it ever so much. But as this was not the time to flinch or show indecision, making up my mind, I said –

'Well, Shebbeare, let me see the men. I'll make a few inquiries first. I will go to the hospital; do you lounge out that way, and let the drummers go round.' As I had been accustomed to visit the hospital about this hour, my going there would excite no suspicion.

In a few minutes I had obtained the information I desired, and found it to be too true that an outbreak was planned for that night. Meanwhile, as the adjutant was looking anxiously at me, I addressed him with these words –

'Now, Shebbeare, will you stand by me?'

'Yes, Colonel,' replied the gallant fellow, 'that I will.'

'Very well; now I'll tell you what I propose to do. In half an hour the men will all assemble in front of their tents for evening roll-call. I will go on parade; and, as there is nothing like facing a difficulty, I'll tax them with their intended outbreak, and we will see what they will do. Tell the officers to look out.'

Accordingly, at sunset I went on parade, assembled the native commissioned and non-commissioned officers in front, at some distance from their respective companies, and taxed them with their intended treachery. As I had expected, the sepoys were utterly confounded when they became aware that their atrocious plot was discovered, and that we had been able to anticipate them. In their confusion, they flatly denied the intended treachery, and swore by all their gods, and by all they held sacred, that they would be 'faithful to their salt', and that no harm would happen to us. The native officers then begged permission to appoint a guard of their own selection to keep watch in the camp at night, as there 'might be some badmashes in the regiment who had entertained the idea of treachery, and it would be as well to guard against it'. I acquiesced in this proposal, though it was a dangerous experiment; but as we were entirely in their hands I thought the best thing we could do was to show, however uneasy we really might be, that we had no fear of them. We felt, indeed, that our only chance of safety was to take things coolly, still seeming to trust the men, and to humour them as much as possible, keeping at the same time a sharp look-out ...

Whilst taxing the native officers with their intended treachery, the men of the different companies were looking on – they were too far off to hear, but they seemed to take their cue from the native officers, who were quiet and very respectful. The European officers, who were also looking on, to my great relief wisely kept at a distance; so that, had anything happened to Shebbeare and myself, they would have had time to escape. Leaving the circle of native officers, I went to each of the companies in succession, and met with the same protestations and vows of fidelity from all, which I took at their proper value – a delay of two or three days, as circumstances might turn out.

As I came from parade after this trying scene, the officers inquired anxiously, 'What is it, colonel – is it all right?'

'Oh, yes,' I replied, as cheerfully as I could; 'I think our throats are safe for tonight, and you may turn in without fear.'

But, though I endeavoured to keep a calm exterior, my mind was anything but at ease, for until I had seen the guard that was to be selected by the native officers, and questioned the adjutant about the men composing it, I could not tell whether they were intended to be our protectors or our executioners! When I saw that the guard and the adjutant had looked through the ranks, I felt more at ease for the night, but my anxiety continued no less for what the coming day might bring forth.

The next and the following days, however, passed quietly enough, but in hourly expectation on our part of news from the force. The regiment meanwhile was so quiet, that I began to hope that the anticipated outbreak would still be delayed for a few days longer, by which time we should surely hear that Delhi had been taken, when all fear of mutiny would be at an end. (S)

In Walker's version of this, his own role is given some prominence:

One day the subadar-major, the senior officer [there were twenty in all], reported to Colonel Seaton that the men intended to mutiny that night and murder the officers, but that there were a number of faithful men who would try and prevent it. The colonel called us all up, and informed us of what had been reported to him. He concluded by saying, 'Now, gentlemen, what do you intend or wish to do?'

'Stick to you, sir,' replied one and all in a breath.

'I shall stick to the regiment as long as feasible,' said the colonel. He then asked who was the orderly officer of the day. I replied that I was. He ordered me at once to visit the guards. I did so and found several men absent from their guards, it being about dusk. I reported this, and ordered the sergeant-major to send other men to replace the absentees.

On returning to my tent, I found my servant taking my bed over the doctor's tent, the largest in camp. On going over there, I found all the officers, except the colonel and Shebbeare the adjutant, assembled, their beds also having been brought there. It was for mutual protection and defence, and would enable us to make a good fight if attacked. Shebbeare and the colonel were going to sleep in the latter's tent just opposite. (W)

The situation regarding the supply of beer and wine was indeed dire, as Robert Shebbeare mentions. Walker notes that the Abdar (man in charge of the drinks) reported that there was only one bottle of beer left. This was put up for auction and amidst much good humour was bought by the doctor, Surgeon-Major Keates, for six rupees – twelve shillings in those days, which was a lot of money!

The actual mutiny of the 60th took place on 10 June (Walker says the 8th, Robert Shebbeare the 9th). From the accounts of Seaton and Walker we get a good idea of the adventures of the two groups of officers which left Rohtuck separately for Delhi. Colonel Seaton's account is reproduced in its entirety, as it casts a lot of light on the conduct of Robert Shebbeare during this episode.

The night of the 9th passed off quietly enough. In the morning I could detect nothing suspicious in camp, or in the countenance or bearing of the men; they were civil and respectful to me personally, as, indeed, they had been throughout, and everything was going on as usual in the line.

Five of the young officers of the regiment made arrangements for going out shooting in the afternoon, and as all seemed quiet, I had no objection. The forenoon passed, and, after luncheon, I sat down to write some letters.

At 4 pm, when I was in the usual hot weather deshabille shirt, loose white cotton drawers, shoes, and stockings, all at once I was startled by a loud explosion, like that of a musket bursting. My first idea was that some accident had happened to one of the young officers who had proposed going out shooting; so, with my pen in my hand, I ran out to see what was the matter, or if anyone was hurt. I could neither hear nor see anything extraordinary; no crowd was assembled anywhere; there were no officers about; not a sound was to be heard; the men were mostly lying down, sleeping after their day's meal; and a few were still cooking or eating. I then went through the centre of the camp towards the cause of the explosion. I could just see the arm-racks in front of the two centre companies, when the havildar-major [native sergeant-major], and several of the sepoys, came rushing up to me. The former, catching me in his arms, said, hurriedly, and with a very agitated voice –

'Colonel, Sahib, don't go to the front.'

'Why not?' I asked.

'The grenadiers are accoutring themselves.'

'Accoutring themselves!' I said. 'By whose order?'

'Biggur-geea our kya.' (They have mutinied; what more can be said?)

The hour for which I had trembled had come at last! I instantly called out for the native officers, especially for one Gungah Persaud, who had been profuse in his vows and protestations, but not one was forthcoming. I then saw that the game was up. The grenadiers, warned by their late failure, had conducted matters so secretly that no intimation of their design had been allowed to ooze out. They had chosen the hour when they knew that most of the sepoys, drowsy after their midday meal, would be asleep in their tents, and they had quietly and silently got together and accoutred themselves in their tent, so that no one might see them. They knew that if muskets were once discharged in mutiny, fear of the consequences would draw nine-tenths of the men into the vortex.

I tried in vain to collect one or two of the native officers. Not one of them answered my appeal. The havildar-major and the sepoys continued to entreat me to be off whilst there was time; so I turned and went towards my tent, and sitting down on the steps of a

41

bungalow close by, I put on a pair of corduroy trousers my servants had brought me. In the meantime our grooms were saddling our horses; some of the officers had already ridden off, and others were preparing to follow, when the sergeant-major rushed past me. A dozen musket-shots were fired at him from the right of the tents, and immediately the whole body of the grenadiers burst out of their tent, firing their muskets as they ran towards us, and shouting with all their might, to rouse the regiment and hurry it into mutiny. In an instant all was confusion. The sleeping men, roused by the unusual noise, started up and stared stupidly about them. Some of them ran into their tents, many to their arms, but not one of the native officers could I see; they all kept out of the way, whether from shame or cowardice I cannot say. The hubbub increased every moment. The shouts of the officers for their grooms and servants, the cries of terror from the camp-followers – some of them were wounded – the galloping of horses, the rush of the people to get out of the way, the fierce shouts of the mutineers, the sharp and frequent reports of the muskets, and the whiz of the balls, may be better imagined than I can describe them.

The sergeant-major was wounded, but Dr Keates took the man up into his dog-cart and drove off at a gallop, in the midst of a shower of bullets and imprecations, for the sergeant was thoroughly hated. In the meantime I rushed into my tent, snatched up my watch and keys, thrust them hurriedly into the breast of my shirt, jumped on my horse and rode off. I had not time to take my sword, for the mutineers were within ten paces of me. The delay of a second more and I might have been bayoneted. Fortunately, the nearest mutineers had discharged their muskets, and, though many were reloading, I managed to escape. I had got a few seconds' start, and in a melee like this a second makes the difference between life and eternity.

I was immediately joined by Lieutenant Shebbeare, and we rode off together. Just outside the camp we overtook Major R. Drought, who was walking, as he had been unable to get on his horse. Shebbeare instantly exclaimed, 'Colonel, the poor old fellow will be murdered. I'll put him on my horse and run for it.' It was a noble and heroic act, and deserves to be recorded.

The major was mounted in all haste and started off, for the musket-balls were now flying pretty sharply about our ears, and the servants and camp-followers were calling out for me to ride for my life.

'Now, Shebbeare,' I said, 'we will ride and die.'

'No, Colonel, I will not; I am young and strong, and I can run.'

'Very well, then, we will keep together.'

So, making him get on the lee side of my horse, he laid hold of the stirrup, and I went off at a round canter. We went on like this for some four hundred yards, when Shebbeare got blown, for he was of a stout habit of body, and unaccustomed to running. So we pulled up and walked quietly along, the mutineers making no attempt to follow us, and their shots now flying wide.

At about eight hundred yards from camp, the road made a slight bend to the left, and the elbow shut out the view of the camp. Here we found the officers assembled, waiting for any who might escape, and hoping that some of the better-disposed sepoys might join them. But the mutineers had provided against this, and had planted a line of sentries along the rear of the camp, to prevent even our servants from accompanying us. One man alone got away, I think his name was Laik Sing; and subsequently half a dozen joined us at camp in Delhi.

The only wounded person was the sergeant-major; the officers were all unhurt. But where, all this time, were our five young comrades who had gone out shooting? What should be done about them? We could not allow them to return to camp, to be murdered, without an attempt to save them; so we moved off the road onto the plain, in sight of the camp, to a spot where we could see through an opening between the camp and the jungle where they had gone to shoot. Thus, when they returned, we should be sure to see them, and one of us would immediately gallop forward, give them timely warning, and bring them off.

For two hours we kept an anxious eye towards the jungle and the camp, looking frequently up and down the road, for it was impossible to forget that we were in a position of great peril. The mutineers might at any moment mount our spare horses and ride out to attack us, or they might cut off our young comrades, if they should meet them before we had time to warn them of the danger to which they were exposed. But they appeared fully occupied in camp, for at intervals sounds of great uproar reached us, with the occasional report of a musket, as if some obnoxious person had been shot down. Presently, too, I saw clouds of smoke ascending. I was glad to see this, for I could tell that they were burning our tents, and immediately after there was a great explosion of ammunition. This explosion, whether the result of accident or design, would at once prevent them from operation immediately in rear of our army, and there seemed to me then to be only two courses left for them – either to return to Umballa and join the 5th NI, which I thought not very likely, or to march to Delhi; and I argued, that by destroying the tents and ammunition, their object was to advance to Delhi by a circuitous route, so as to avoid all chance of a collision with our troops. In this case they would naturally destroy the tents, which they could not take on without encumbering their march; and of ammunition they would find abundance in the Delhi magazine.

At sunset I addressed the officers. 'Gentlemen,' I said, 'we have done our duty by our comrades and must now do our duty by our commander-in-chief. We must join him as soon as we can, and let him know the possibility of having an enemy in his rear. My plan is to go at a foot's pace all night, so as to reach the vicinity of Delhi by daybreak, when we must find out where our camp is and be guided by circumstances.'

We started accordingly, not in a very happy frame of mind, but glad enough to have escaped so far with our lives. We were mortified exceedingly at the failure of our endeavours to keep the regiment together and preserve it from the crime of mutiny. We had certainly done our best, but it was nevertheless inexpressibly annoying to have failed, even while we were forced to acknowledge that from the first the task which we had undertaken was hopeless.

In the meantime we were still harassed by many uncertainties and perplexities, and there were several important questions which we were unable to solve. Where would we find the camp? Was the country about Delhi as ill-disposed as it was about Rohtuck? And that was very bad indeed. Mr Lock, the collector of Rohtuck, accompanied me to Paneeput; and shortly after our arrival at Rohtuck, on sending to some of his villages for the arrears of revenue, the people replied that they would pay it when they saw our power re-established. Let it be borne in mind that the people of this part of the country had cut off some of our stragglers and intercepted our posts, and that from this district came numbers of our irregular cavalry soldiers, who were one and all thoroughly disaffected.

We kept on all night at a moderate pace, stopping only towards morning to get a drink of water at a village. It was a large place, and the people crowded around us, anxious to know whence we came and who we were. I told them that we were going to Delhi and that our regiment was close behind. They were civil enough, gave us water to drink, and told us some gentlemen had just passed through.

About three in the morning we heard a horseman coming along. Who could it be? We drew up and challenged. It was a sowar (trooper) from Hodson's Horse with a letter for the Colonel.

I read the note by the light of a cigar vehemently smoked by one of the officers. It was to the effect that our troops had met the rebels at Budlee ka Serai, on the morning of the 8th, had beaten them, captured their guns, driven them from their positions on the ridge above the cantonment into Delhi, and that the camp was pitched in the cantonments. So now we were all right. We knew exactly where to find the camp, and what to do. And, above all, it was cheering to hear that the rebels had been beaten. So we rode on with lighter hearts. At daybreak we reached a village not far from Delhi, and were going through it, when the head man came out with some of the villagers and warned us that the rebels had possession of the bridge on the canal on that road, but he would send two men to show us the way round by another bridge, which would bring us to camp by the Kurnaul road. We were very thankful for this; the men guided us safely, and a little after 9 am I dismounted at Sir H. Barnard's tent. (S)

Walker's version of the events of the last afternoon at Rohtuck is puzzlingly different from Seaton's:

On June 8th, in the afternoon, five of us, the junior officers of the regiment, went out shooting, and were just about to return to camp when we met some of the bandsmen, who were escaping from it. They told us that the corps had mutinied and murdered all the officers, and that a company was coming out to hunt us up. We met others who corroborated the report. We youngsters were well up in the topography of the Rohtuck district, having studied the map well. After a few minutes consultation we made for the Delhi road, determining to ride along it towards the camp, hoping to pick up some of the other officers. To our delight we found them all on the road unhurt, except the sergeant-major, who had been shot through the arm. All the officers except Lieut-Colonel R. Drought had got their horses; Doctor Keates had even brought away his dogcart, in which he had for some days kept his valuables. The sergeant-major was seated on the dogcart, his arm having been bound up.

After a few minutes' delay, during which the colonel was in conversation with some of the men who had remained faithful to us, we five juniors started on our ride to join the Delhi Field Force. We soon got on ahead of all the others, delighted at the idea of our emancipation, and eager to get on. The road was fearfully dusty, for not a drop of rain had fallen for months, and the heat was intense. We were soon begrimed with dust and parched with thirst, as were our horses, although we had not ridden them fast. The inhabitants of the villages which were on the roadside as we passed freely expressed their hatred of us, and after passing one village we had a shot fired at us. (W)

According to Walker, he and the other four young officers then had a very adventurous journey on their way to Delhi, and were deliberately given wrong directions by one of the villagers which put them into the path of a body of mutineers, which they managed, however, to evade. Later, at another fork in the road, they were told by a man in a bungalow nearby that they should on no account go right, or they would run into a band of rebels. After their previous experience, they thought that they should go against his advice, but, as it turned out, he had been telling the truth, and they promptly ran into the rebels he had warned them about!

In the morning they arrived at Delhi.

Soon after entering the camp we met the General, Sir Henry Barnard. Being the senior of the party, I went up to him and reported the mutiny of the regiment, and the safety, we hoped, of all the other officers. The General replied that he never expected to see one of us again, and expressed his joy at our escape. We went straight to the tents of the 1st Fusiliers, where we were enthusiastically received, and right hospitably treated. (W)

I went in to make my report, and found him at breakfast with his staff, perfectly acquainted with the mutiny of the 60th, but surprised to see me. This struck me as very extraordinary, but it was soon explained. When the regiment mutinied, some servants ran out into the jungle and warned our young comrades, whom we believed lost, telling them that the sepoys had mutinied, with the addition of some dreadful story of our having been murdered. On being thus alarmed they had taken to their horses, and had cut into the road to Delhi some two or three miles ahead of us. Towards morning, whilst they were drinking water at the village where we subsequently stopped, they saw us coming, and believing us to be sepoys mounted on our horses in chase of them, they galloped off, burst through the rebel picket in possession of the bridge above-mentioned, wheeled sharp off to the left, and got into camp, where they told the tale of the mutiny of the 60th, their wonderful escape, and our sad fate. (S)

Notes

1 Walker, Colonel, T.N., *Through the Mutiny. Reminiscences of 30 Years Active Service and Sport in India (1854–66)*, Gibbings and Co., London, 1907.

2 Seaton, Major General Sir Thomas, KCB, *From Cadet to Colonel. The Record of a Life of Active Service*, Hurst and Blackett, London, 1866.

3 State Papers, I. 278. In David, *The Indian Mutiny, 1857*.

Chapter Three

THE SIEGE OF DELHI, JUNE–SEPTEMBER, 1857

When, on 11 June, Robert Shebbeare arrived at the British camp outside Delhi, the city had been in rebel hands for a month, having been overwhelmed by the insurgents on 11 May; many soldiers, together with their wives and children, had been massacred. The British camp to the north-west had been taken over by the mutineers and the remnants of the British garrison had escaped as best they could (see David, 2002, Chapter 9, for a good account).

On 7 June the two elements of the Delhi Field Force (one under General Sir Henry Barnard, from Ambala; the other commanded by Brigadier Archdale Wilson, from Meerut) had met at Alipore, not far from Delhi, and together they defeated a large concentration of rebel troops at Badli-ki-Serai on the 8th. After driving the enemy from the ridge overlooking the city, they took up positions at various points along it, which were to be the focus of constant attack for the next three months.

Continuation of letter of 11th July, to his mother:

Brigadier Showers, who commands the first brigade, asked me to act as his orderly officer (a sort of aide-de-camp) and I was very glad to accept his offer. I served under him for three days and in one smart action on the heights I could not but admire his extreme coolness and steadiness under fire. I should have liked to remain with him very much but was offered the acting appointment of 2nd in command of the Guide Corps and the Brigadier advised me to accept it. Indeed, it was too good an offer to refuse. It is a wonderful regiment composed of eight companies of infantry and three troops of cavalry. The men are from all countries. One company of Peshawar, another from the country between Peshawar and Cabool and then a company of Sikhs and another from Nepaul (Ghoorkhas) and they are armed with rifles and dressed in dust-coloured clothes. The natives call us the Khakee Pultan or Dusty Regiment from the colour of the uniform. They are capital men and do their work most pluckily, adding every day to their former fame. The present commandant, Hodson, is an old friend of mine and we get on very well together. He takes the cavalry and I command the infantry in the field. The men are getting to know me now and we shall get on very well together. I can speak to the Sikhs in their own language and, if I remain with them long, I shall pick up Pooshtoo from the Cabool people, I doubt not.

We have had several very sharp engagements and lost a very large number of men. For three days we have been more quiet. I can't tell when there is a chance of Delhi falling; we have so small a number of men that it appears to be thought imprudent to attack. They attack us on the heights every two or three days, but are of course always repulsed with great loss. On the 10th June we drove them back to within 250 yards of the Cabool Gate, into which they retired in a great disorder. As I escaped from camp without any servants or traps I am not very well furnished with clothes, but I manage to get on wonderfully well and I am very happy. Pray imagine my dress, for I cannot send a sketch of it. A straw hat of this shape, covered with a turban of dust-coloured loose kind of cloth of the same colour, and lower were garments of the same prevailing hue, met by leather shooting gaiters. This, with a native sword, a water bottle and a haversack completed my working costume. I hope to send you a sketch some day.

We are always quartered at Hindoo Rao's house on the heights opposite the city. We have a very good room which we share with such officers of the Royal Rifles as may be on picket. They are a nice set of fellows, thorough gentlemen, and we get on capitally together. Our men and the riflemen are very fond of being together and always address one another as 'Brudder'. They can't understand one another but have long conversations, each talking in his own language, and by the help of signs and gesticulations they get on satisfactorily to both parties, if we may judge by the hearty laughs and slaps on the shoulder with which they wind up.

Pray address me in future as 2nd in Command Guide Corps, Delhi Field Force.

Robert H. Shebbeare

49

Robert Shebbeare was appointed second in command of the Guide Corps, which had a legendary reputation for courage throughout the army in India, on 13 June.

> The Guides and Goorkhas were adept in skirmishing; their being on our side was one of the hundred chances which saved us from utter destruction. Trained in danger from infancy, among the robber tribes of his frontier, the Afghan soldier was more than a match for the Poorbeah. The name of Patan (Pathan) or Conquerer, which is given in India to the native of Cabool and his descendants, was a proof of his superiority.[1]

'Too much cannot be said in praise of the Guides Corps. Of native regiments they are second to none. Their services on the Peshawar frontier, and in various parts of the Punjaub, has gained them a well-earned reputation in India.'[2]

The Guide Corps was formed in 1846, and the uniform, described with amusement by Robert Shebbeare, was introduced by Hodson in 1847, on the recommendation of Sir Henry Lawrence, as being a much more suitable dress for fighting than those worn by other native regiments. The latter were often clothed in European-style clothing, quite unsuitable to the climate and their own traditions of dress, which caused a good deal of rancour amongst the sepoys.

William Hodson (1821–58), like Nicholson, was a person of great ability who attracted admiration from some and aroused antipathy in others. He was educated at Rugby under Arnold and went on to Trinity College, Cambridge, where he took his degree in 1844. Finding himself prone to headaches brought on by close work he decided to join the HEIC army and went out to India in 1845, where he had connections to a number of people of influence. He managed from the start to get himself noticed and into places where the action was; his forthright and lucid opinions about the state of the army, and a capacity to get a lot of work done efficiently, soon brought him to the attention of his superiors. Through the patronage of Henry Lawrence he was appointed second-in-command of the newly formed Guide Corps, and distinguished himself as a fearless and thinking soldier with a capacity to inspire his men. After a spell of civil duties, which was considered to be part of the career path of ambitious soldiers, he returned to the Guides as Commandant, over the heads of several officers more

Hindoo Rao's house from the observatory.

Hindoo Rao's house.

Bridge of boats over the River Jumna.

The Metcalfe Stables Picket.

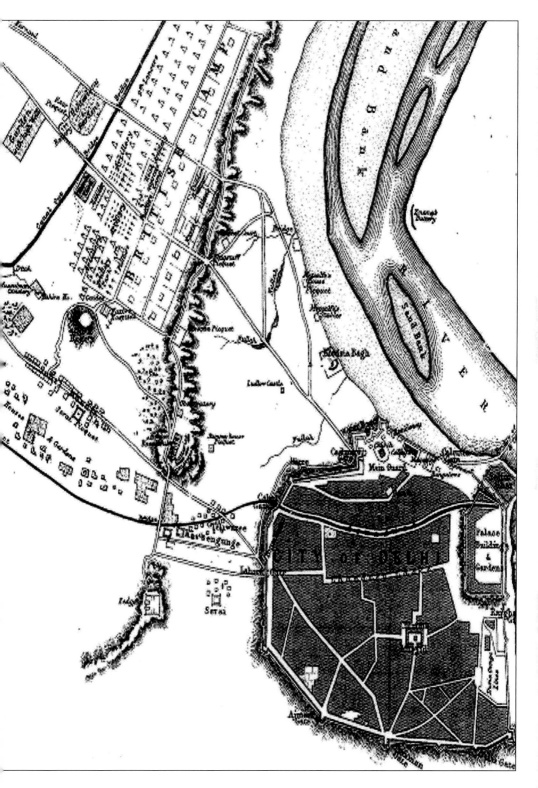

Map of Delhi.

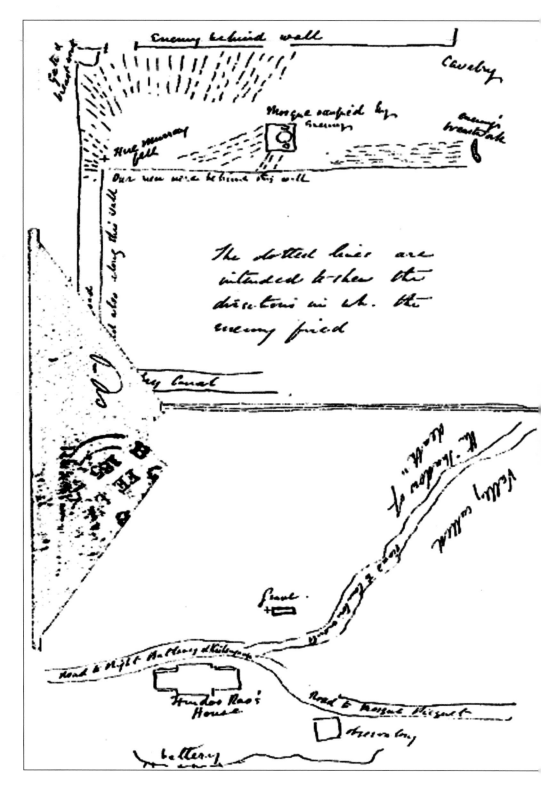

Sketch map of enemy positions (with Hindu Rao's house at the bottom).

Officers of the 15th Punjab Regiment. Robert Shebbeare is seated, 2nd from right, middle row.

Native officers and men of the 15th Punjab Regiment, 1860.

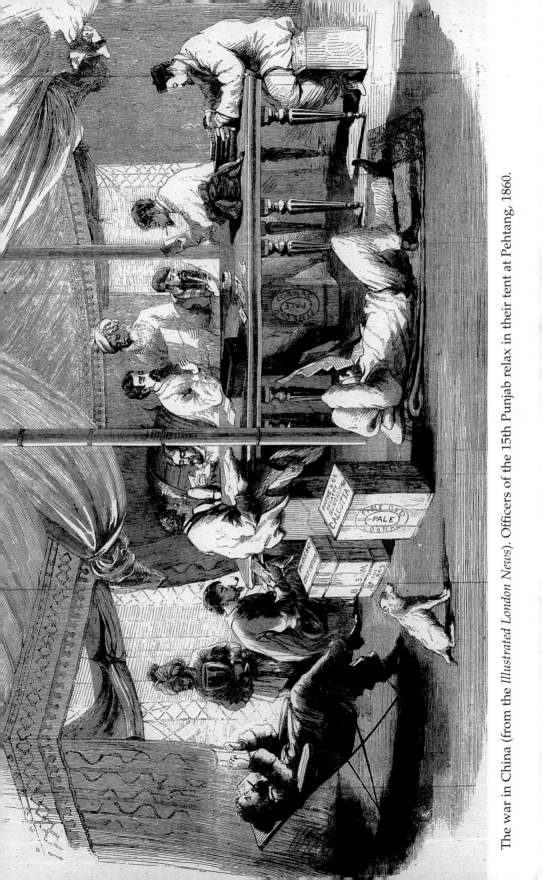

The war in China (from the *Illustrated London News*). Officers of the 15th Punjab relax in their tent at Pehtang, 1860.

Charles John

Louisa Matilda

Charles Hooper

Henry Francis

Margaretta Louisa

Helen Charlotte

Reginald John

Alice Mary

Robert Shebbeare's parents and siblings *c.* 1860.

senior to him. This, together with a tendency to be overzealous in pushing through his ideas, seems to have made him many enemies, some of whom plotted against him; he was brought before a court of enquiry in 1855 for irregularities in the regimental accounts for which he was eventually exonerated, but which at the time threatened to end his career.

At the outbreak of the mutiny his undoubted talents were soon put to good use again and in May 1857, General Anson, the C-in-C, asked him to raise a regiment of irregular cavalry, which came to be known as Hodson's Horse, and also to be in charge of the Intelligence Department of the Delhi Field Force. He was constantly in the thick of the fighting during the siege of Delhi and afterwards, with a small force, went out to capture, first the King of Delhi, and then his sons, whom he personally executed. With his regiment he was involved in numerous mopping-up operations and was killed during the successful recapture of Lucknow on 11 March 1858. For further reading, see Hodson, G.H., *Twelve Years of a Soldier's Life in India: Being Extracts from the Letters of the Late Major W.S.R. Hodson*, London, 1859.

'Hodson rejected the tight scarlet uniform of the regulars in favour of baggy smocks and pyjama trousers. And to make the Guides "invisible in a land of dust" these were treated with a dye from a local dwarf palm to produce a yellow-green colour, known in Hindustani as "khaki", or "dust-coloured".'[3]

On 13 May 1857, the Guides had been ordered to help suppress the mutineers who had taken over in Delhi and Captain Daly, in Hodsen's absence in Kandahar, marched the Guides from Hoti Mardan to join the Delhi Field Force. On the way they were delayed by action from rebels at Karnal and other places but managed to get to Delhi on 9 June, having covered a distance of 580 miles in twenty-six days.[4]

Before they had had time to pitch their tents they were almost immediately in a fierce action in which all the officers received wounds.

Camp before Delhi, July 25th, 1857

My dearest mother,

The mail leaves for England tomorrow and I must write a few lines as you will probably see my name amongst the wounded. I am thankful to be able to tell you that although I was struck by three

51

bullets my wounds are very slight, so much so that although only eleven days have elapsed since I was hit I hope to go on duty again tomorrow. One ball hit me on the right side, another almost simultaneously on the muscle of the right arm and a third about five minutes after on the right arm above the wrist.

We are still before Delhi with the small force originally assembled, so that we are unable to attack the place, but manage to beat back the mutineers on every occasion, sometimes to the very walls of the city. They have attacked the right of our position near Hindoo Rao's place twenty-two times! I have been present in nearly every engagement. The weather is very unfavourable for a standing camp as it rains heavily every two or three days. However, we live when on duty at the Rao's house and are well sheltered. Since I have been on the sick list I have been living with some officers of the 60th Royal Rifles who were old acquaintances and who have been very kind to me. I have been very fortunate in getting appointed 2nd in command of a new Sikh cavalry regiment raised by Hodson, 1st Fusiliers, an old friend, and in getting my old chum Baker into the same. As I am only acting in the Guides I am glad to have this appointment to fall back upon when the officer whose place I hold rejoins. However, Daly, who commands them, tells me not to give up the Guides on any account as it will be better for me to remain with them. He said that he was not at liberty to tell me why but he 'knew it was the best thing I could do'. He also said he thought I should get command of a regiment after the present campaign and that he would do his best to get it for me. So you will see that I am a lucky fellow.

I have kept no particular account of the doings before Delhi and therefore hope you will see a good history in the overland paper. I had intended to keep a journal but at first I had so much to do that I could not find time and then I thought it hardly worthwhile to begin.

The doctor has just been here and promises to let me go on duty tomorrow if it does not rain. I am anxiously looking for a small box of clothes from Umballah for at present I have no warm clothing at all and flannels will be a great comfort to me. I luckily left two cricketing suits at Umballah which I hope to receive in a day or two.

I hope I find you well and happy at home and please believe in my sincere good wishes to all. I hope you would have received some of my former letters. I have written frequently since the disturbances commenced and sent my letters by all sorts of different routes.

Believe me my dearest mother ever your most affectionate son

Robert H. Shebbeare

On 12 June, the rebels made various attacks but were beaten off. As temporary aide to Brigadier Showers for three days, Robert Shebbeare would have been involved in the skirmishes with rebel troops in the broken ground near Metcalfe House, and in the setting up of two pickets, known as the 'Stable' and 'Cowshed' pickets, to guard the British left flank.

For the first two months after their arrival, until sufficient reinforcements got through to help, it was the British troops, rather than the Indian rebels, who were under siege, as the field force had insufficient strength to make an assault on Delhi, and the almost daily actions consisted mainly of attacks on the British positions on the ridge. Hindoo Rao's house, in which Robert Shebbeare saw duty from June to September, was the most fiercely contested point of the British position.

From a number of other accounts, it is possible to get a good idea of some of the many engagements in which Robert Shebbeare was involved, and to appreciate the appalling conditions in which the soldiers were living and fighting.

> In the first six weeks of the siege, night or day no man undressed, except for a few minutes, for the necessary ablutions, and this was not always possible. We lay down in our clothes, with accoutrements either on or by our sides, ready to slip on the moment the alarm was sounded.
>
> The heat was fearful; yet day after day we had to stand for hours in sun and hot wind, or, worst of all, to endure the torture of lying down on the burning rocks on the ridge – baked by them on one side, while the sun was 'doing the other'. In this position many an officer and man, struck by the sun and unable to rise, was carried off to hospital delirious and raving. The flies were in myriads, and added to our torment; they clung to our faces; they dabbed at every part of the body that was exposed; they covered our food until it was uneatable, and worried us incessantly until dusk. As the siege went on, and the bodies of men and the carcasses of animals accumulated, lying exposed in places where there was no soil, so we could not bury them, these pests increased in numbers and irritating powers, and made us fully comprehend the awfulness of the plague of flies. The thermometer ranged in our tent as high as 115 degrees, and constant exposure to the sun and wind that produced this great heat in the shade, began to fill our hospitals rapidly with cases of sunstroke, fever and dysentery. (Seaton, 1866)

Walker was attached by now to the 2nd Fusiliers.

There were no helmets in those days. We had no better protection from the sun than forage caps made from pasteboard, with a small white turban neatly folded around them, with one end hanging down neatly but uselessly behind, with black leather peaks. The men had wadded covers and curtains, which were worse.' (Walker, 1907)

There was a severe cannonade from the enemy on 17 June, and an officer was killed and many were wounded at Hindoo Rao's House.

On 19 June, a large number of rebels poured out of the city and a general alarm was sounded. They disappeared among the gardens in Kissengunge and it was thought that they had gone out foraging. The troops stood by for several hours in the hot sun and eventually were stood down. Not long before sunset, the sound of gunfire from the rear of the camp roused everyone again and it was realized that the camp was being attacked from the rear. Twelve guns and the available cavalry under Brigadier Hope Grant were sent to met them and a sharp action ensued. The enemy infantry and artillery did a lot of damage, and part of the 9th Lancers and the Guide Cavalry made a charge at the enemy. Brevet Lieutenant Colonel Yule was killed and Captain Daly, Commandant of the Guide Corps, was severely wounded. Hodson took over as Commandant, leading the cavalry, with Robert Shebbeare second in command, in charge of the three companies of Guide infantry.

'The next event that I recollect took place on June 23rd, although between the 12th and that time the alarm was constantly sounded and fighting took place, but the 23rd was a record day.' (Walker, op. cit.)

The 23rd of June was a particularly busy day and was significant, from the British point of view, in that it was the centenary of the Battle of Plassey, when the East India Company troops under Clive had defeated 50,000 native troops with 3,000 men, and had begun their long period of supremacy as the agents of the British government. Intelligence from Delhi suggested that the rebels would make an all-out assault on the British positions on that day, as they had been promised by both Hindu and Moslem leaders that on this date, being an important one in the calendar of both religions, the foreign invaders would be overthrown, and native rule restored.

As is often the case in comparing the accounts of any military event, times, numbers of casualties and other pieces of detail vary from author to author, though the gist of what happened on that day seems to have been agreed by all.

It was very well known in our camp, that we should have a hard struggle for existence; perhaps our weak force would be annihilated under the swarms of the enemy. The day before, everyone thought anxiously of the morrow; some thought wistfully of their wives and children in the hills, some made their wills; the more religious said their prayers.

About three o'clock in the morning a cannonade was opened from the walls, and their whole force came out, and occupied the Subzi Mundi and Kissengunge. From these points they could enfilade both our camp and batteries. (Unknown officer)

During the course of the day, the rebels made many attempts to attack Hindoo Rao's, but each time they were repulsed. 'The heat was terrific, and constantly on the increase until the afternoon. The sun, pouring down flames, aided by the wind, which was hot like the blast from a furnace, struck down numbers of our officers and men, who were carried off to hospital.' (Seaton, op. cit.)

At four in the afternoon the battle was still in progress with unabated vigour, when another course was taken: an order was issued to the Rifles, Gorkhas, and Guides, to carry the Subzi Mundi, which they did in right gallant style, despite their eleven hours of previous labour and exposure to the sun, and want of refreshment. The enemy were driven by them from wall to bank, and from bank to wall. Now, the sepoys ascended the tops of houses, of which there were many in the immediate neighbourhood, but their tenure of them only lasted for the few moments which it took our brave troops to reach them; numbers of the enemy began to fall, and several of our brave fellows beside them. The mutineers retired within the walls about six in the evening, finding to their chagrin that their prophets were a living lie, and had woefully deceived them. (Rotton, 1866)

The Pandies had been the attacking party all morning, and now came our turn. The column at once dispersed the rebels on our right flank, and then advanced towards Subzee Mundee. A rush was made at the Serai and Sammy House, and both were carried, every rebel in them being put to death. (Seaton, op. cit.)

By nightfall, the rebels had retreated to within the walls of Delhi in a state of some demoralization, and the British gained some momentum by establishing pickets at the Sammy House and the serai in Subzi Mundi.

This (the first three weeks) was undoubtedly the most trying period of the whole siege, from the constant demands made on our services, and the frequent and long exposure to the tremendous heat day after day. The days were at their longest and the heat at its greatest, our numbers at their lowest, and the enemy's courage and activity at their highest. (Seaton, op. cit.)

On 27 June the rains started and, as with most things in life, it brought mixed blessings. On the one hand daytime temperatures were not quite so extreme, and sleep at night became more comfortable; but on the other, movement of men and supplies was more difficult. It also brought with it an outbreak of cholera and, during July in particular, a large number of men in certain regiments died from it, including Sir Henry Barnard, the commander of the Delhi Field Force. Many others were stricken with dysentery and 'fever', presumably malaria.

We hear mention of Robert Shebbeare in Hodson's diary for July 2:

I have been quite unable to write since the 29th, on the night of which I was ordered off again to Bhagput, to try to bring the boats down to camp, either to make a bridge here or a 'stop' for the enemy. I expected to be back in good time on the 30th, but the wind and waves were against me, and I could not get my fleet of boats down the river.

Shebbeare was with me, and we worked like a couple of 'navvies', passing the two days and one night on the banks of the river, without shelter, and almost without food, for we had nothing but a couple of 'chupatties' each, and a small tin of soup and a little tea, which I fortunately took with me. Poor Shebbeare would soon lose the graceful rotund of his figure if he were long on such short commons, but I do not think any amount of starvation could reduce my horizontal dimensions. All's well that ends well, however, and we succeeded in getting every boat safe into camp last night.[5]

At the beginning of July there was a period of relative quietness, until on the 9th, while enemy cavalry were attacking the camp from the rear, Hindoo Rao's received a severe bombardment and many positions were attacked, including the Sammy House, where young Murray distinguished himself and was again wounded.

The infantry of the Guides also greatly distinguished themselves this day under Lieutenants E.E.B. Bond and A.W. Murray, who, with seventy-eight men held a breastwork against far superior numbers of the enemy advancing towards them. The Guides had run out of ammunition, of which the enemy appeared to be equally short. And the fight was carried on with stones, until Lieutenant H. de Brett, then attached to the Guides, arrived with a reinforcement of fifty bayonets and, charging the enemy in the flank, so bewildered them that they broke and fled. Some idea of the numbers of the enemy and the losses inflicted on him may be gauged from the fact that ninety of his dead were counted about the breastwork. On this day the Guides' casualties were Lieutenant Murray and twenty-seven other ranks killed and wounded.[6]

As many of the other young officers who were attached to the Guides (Murray, McLean and Bond in particular) are mentioned in Robert Shebbeare's correspondence, details of some of their exploits have also been included, to give a sense of the camaraderie that pertained, and of the constant dangers in which they found themselves.

On the same day that Murray and Bond were distinguishing themselves, Robert Shebbeare was in action with the Guides, as Major Reid recalls in his memoirs:

Away I went with five companies of my own regiment (The Sirmoor Battalion of Gurkhas), two companies 60th Rifles under Sir E. Campbell and 180 of the Guides under Shebbeare, in all about 750 men. We drove the enemy before us through the jungle and down the Grand Trunk Road, where they were posted in thousands. We got to within 250 yards of the walls ... Twenty Guides killed or wounded ... Our spies say losses very great.[7]

On 14 July, when Robert Shebbeare was three times wounded, a large force of the enemy attacked the batteries at Hindoo Rao's. A column under Brigadier Showers was sent to clear the enemy back and Hodson gives a detailed account of the action in his diary.

The fight on that day (14th) was the old story. An attack in force on the right of our position; the enemy are allowed to blaze away, expending powder, and doing us no harm, until 4 p.m., when a column was sent down to turn them out of the gardens and villages they had occupied, and drive them back to the city. I had just returned from a long day's work with the cavalry, miles away in the rear, and had come back as far as Light's advanced battery. I was chatting with him for a few minutes en passant, when I saw the column pass down. I joined it, and sent for a few horsemen to accompany me, and when we got under fire, I found the Guide Infantry, under Shebbeare, had been sent to join in the attack. I accompanied them, and while the Fusiliers and Coke's men were driving the mass of the enemy helter-skelter through the gardens to our right, I went, with the Guides, Goorkhas, and part of the Fusiliers, along the Grand Trunk Road leading right into the gates of Delhi. We were exposed to a heavy fire of grape from the walls, and musketry from behind trees and rocks; but pushing on, we drove them right up to the very walls, killing uncounted numbers, and then we were ordered to retire. This was done too quickly by the artillery, and some confusion ensued, the troops hurrying back too fast. The consequence was, the enemy rallied, bringing up infantry, then a large body of cavalry, and behind them two guns to bear on us. There were very few of our men, but I managed to get eight horsemen to the front. Shebbeare, though wounded, aided me in rallying some Guide Infantry, and Greville and Jacob (whose horse had been shot) coming up, brought a few scattered Fusiliers forward. I called on the men to fire, assuring them that the body of cavalry coming down would never stand; my gallant Guides stood their ground like men; Shebbeare, Greville, Jacob and little Butler, came to the front, and the mass of the enemy's cavalry, just as I said, stopped, reeled, turned, and fled in confusion; the guns behind them were for the moment deserted, and I tried hard to get up a charge to capture them; we were within thirty paces; twenty-five resolute men would have been enough; but the soldiers were blown, and could not push on in the face of such odds, unsupported as we were, for the whole of the rest of the troops had retired. My eight horsemen stood their ground, and the little knot of officers used every exertion to aid us, when suddenly two rascals rushed forward with lighted portfires in their hands, fired the guns, loaded with grape, in our faces, and when the smoke cleared away, we found, to our infinite disgust and chagrin, that they had limbered up the guns and were off at a gallop. We then had to effect our retreat to rejoin the column, under a heavy fire of grape and musketry, and many men and officers were hit in doing it. I managed to get the Guides to retire quietly, fighting as they went, and fairly checking the enemy, on which I galloped back and brought up two guns, when we stopped all opposition, and drove the last living rebel into his Pandemonium. My Guides stood firm, and as well as my new men, behaved admirably.

During this time Hodson had been raising an irregular cavalry regiment, which became famous as 'Hodson's Horse', an on 17 July he wrote: 'For officers, I hope to have permanently, Macdowell, Shebbeare (now acting as my 2nd in command of the Guides, and an excellent officer), and Hugh Gough of the 3rd Cavalry.'

From 14 to 25 July, Robert Shebbeare was on the sick list, but at the end of the month, Hodson having left to take command of his new regiment, Hodson's Horse, he became acting Commandant of the Guides. By now reinforcements had been arriving to strengthen the Delhi Field Force, the actions of the enemy became less frequent, and much of the aggravation came from the rains, boredom and the effects of disease. It can be seen from Robert Shebbeare's letter of 10 August that the month was frustrating and tedious as the build-up to an assault on Delhi slowly gathered pace. A bullet through his hat near the Sammy House on the 9th was the highlight of his activities.

Despatch, Aug.12, 1857, Major Reid to Brigadier General Wilson. Main Picket, Hindoo Rao's House, Aug 12. My dear General, – My report of the attack on my position on the night of the 1st and morning of the 2nd instant was a hurried affair; but I am glad indeed you have given me an opportunity of bringing to notice the names of officers and men who have served under me since the 8th June last. I cannot speak too highly of the conduct of the detachment of the 60th Royal Rifles, who have on all occasions behaved admirably, and ever maintained the reputation of their distinguished corps. Would wish to bring to your notice the names of two officers of this regiment, viz., Captain Sir E. Campbell and Captain J.R. Wilson, who have at different times commanded the parties on duty at this post, and from whom I have always received the greatest assistance. Both are most excellent officers and I beg to recommend them to notice. My acknowledgements are due to Lieutenant R.H. Shebbeare, now commanding the distinguished Corps of Guides, who has been three times slightly wounded while on duty with me here; also to Lieutenant Hawes, Adjutant (likewise wounded), and other officers doing duty with the corps.

Amongst the Shebbeare Papers are some undated notes in pencil from Major Charles Reid, who commanded the picket at Hindoo Rao's House throughout the siege, which give some idea of the fluidity of the situation, and of the incisiveness needed to deal rapidly with the constant attacks. To handle these tangible, and in many ways very moving pieces of history, written in the heat of battle, makes the events become vividly real in a way that it is difficult to recapture in print.

My dear Shebbeare, Read the accompanying in case of attack. Kindly take the remainder of your men (twenty Gh?) to the Sammy House and take command of that post. More men will be required behind the breast work on the right of Sammy House. At present there are only fifty of my men there. We have a working party out on the left of the Sammy House. Look out for them please. Let the Rifle Officers know of the expected attack.

Yours sincerely, C. Reid

My dear Shebbeare,
Look out, they are turning out again.
   The whole force is out.
Sincerely,
C. Reid

My dear Shebbeare, I have been at the breastwork all night ready to support you – Kissengunge is full of rascals, and they have during the night erected a battery for three heavy guns in the very place where I destroyed their batteries on the 17th June. One gun is already in position and has fired three shots. The other two will open immediately.
   We must attack them or we shall soon be broken out of this.

Yes, by all means give your men a talk of pay. I'll write to Flowers.
Have you a flag at Hindoo Rao's?

Yes, of course you have.

Sincerely,

C. Reid

Camp before Delhi. August 10th, 1857

My dear Harry,

Here we are, still before Delhi, and we are getting very tired of the affair. For want of troops we have been obliged to remain inactive, contenting ourselves with repelling the attacks of the mutineers, and getting quietly shot at in our own trenches. I'll give you a sketch of our position on the opposite side, which will enable you to understand somewhat about our movements. I suppose you will get full accounts of the various fights in the overland papers, so I will give news only of myself. I got a bullet through my hat yesterday while passing along the breastwork near the 'Sammy House' where I was on picket. It gave me a bad headache and slightly cut the skin, but no more. I have such a bad memory that I don't know what I told you in my last letter.

Sketch of the British positions before Delhi

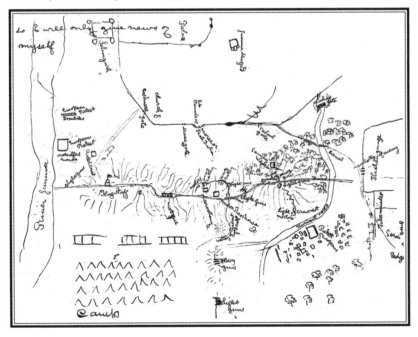

Did I tell you that I am acting as commandant of the Corps of Guides? I am so and shall probably be so if I live another month or two. We expect reinforcements daily, very strong ones, and then we shall quickly make an end of this wretched city. I shall be very glad when the siege is over as it is very tiresome and very hard work, and Delhi very unhealthy at the end of the rains. I have only been able to snatch half an hour to scribble this note and am off again to the picket.

With best love to father and mother and all at home.

yours affectionately

Robert H. Shebbeare

The road to the camp from Hindoo Rao's House is marked 'Valley of the Shadow of Death' as there were many casualties there from shells fired by the Indian heavy batteries.

Camp Delhi 26th August, 1857 9.30 am

My dearest mother,

I have only just heard (being on picket) that the mail goes out today at 10 am and have just time to tell you that I am all safe. General Nicholson got twelve guns from the enemy this morning.[8] I cannot write another line or I shall lose the mail.

Ever your most affectionate son, Robert H. Shebbeare

Camp before Delhi Sept 11th, 1857

My dearest mother,

I have just come down to camp from the picket and hear that there are doubts about letters posted tomorrow being in time, so I have borrowed writing materials from Innes, who lives in camp, to scribble a few lines and that I am alive, hearty and happy. Our siege train having arrived, we are hard at work battering the walls down and I suppose the breach will be practicable by the day after tomorrow when I hope we shall get in and make an end of the business. Innes is quite well and will write to his mother tomorrow.

I have had a disagreeable attack of fever but believe I have got over it. A move away from Delhi will do us all an immense deal of good as we all require a change of air. I wish the mail could be kept for three or four days that I might tell you the end of the business, but you must remain in suspense until the next mail I fear. I hope my letter will find you all well and happy at home and that you will believe me to be ever your most affectionate son.

Robert H. Shebbeare

Delhi September 30th, 1857

My dearest mother,

I am again obliged to send you a shabby chit as I have been out of the district on an expedition, but as you will again see my name amongst the list of wounded I cannot leave you without the assurance that my wound was very slight and that it did not prevent my bringing the regiment out of action – we had very severe fighting. Poor young Murray, as fine a young soldier as I ever met, close by my side. A great number were killed and wounded and our loss especially was very heavy but thank God the day was won and we are now living inside the city. The mutineers have entirely disappeared from before Delhi and we have just heard of a victory gained against them by Colonel Greathed at Boolandsluckur. We shall have plenty of troops shortly and I doubt not everything will be settled. My own prospects are heightening considerably but my loss of friends has been very great. I have had no letters from home for two months and am longing for news of you all. With sincere love to all,

believe me dearest mother, your most affectionate son

Robert H. Shebbeare

Many of the events at the time of the storming of Delhi on 14 September have been exhaustively covered by others and there are a great many accounts of heroic exploits, particularly at the Cashmere Gate; but a brief account of the general picture might be helpful at this point.

During the early part of the campaign, the British, through want of sufficient forces, were mostly engaged in repelling attacks by large numbers of rebels on their positions along the ridge.

In the first part of September, when a siege train and other reinforcements arrived from the Punjab, it was decided to mount a full-scale siege, and the artillery batteries began to throw a daily barrage at the walls, a softening-up process that was concentrated on the north side of the city, where the main assault was to take place.

The assault force was divided into four columns, with one in reserve, each with specific objectives: the first column, under Brigadier Nicholson, was to storm the breach near the Cashmere Bastion; the second, under Brigadier Jones, was to storm the breach in the water bastion; the third, under Colonel Sir Edward Campbell, was to blow open the Cashmere Gate and storm the breach; the fourth column, under Major Reid, was to attack the suburb of Kissengunge and enter the Lahore Gate on the eastern wall of the city.[9]

The actions of the fourth column, in which Robert Shebbeare commanded the Guide infantry, have received much less attention than those of the other three, perhaps with good reason, as it did not achieve military success, although it did serve to divert large numbers of rebel troops from the walls of the city. The suburb of Kissengunge had been a persistent source of irritation to the British flank throughout the early campaign, and because of the nature of the terrain, and the shelter that the walls and gardens offered to small groups of rebels, guerrilla warfare by the infantry was the order of the day, as the cavalry could not function in these conditions. This indeed proved to be the case on the day itself, when the cavalry in support of the column, under Brigadier Hope Grant, had to remain still under heavy fire for some two hours, as they were unable to deploy.

Rotton (op. cit.) gives much detail as to how the columns were organized and how Major Reid's plan was intended to work, but it was thwarted by the usual mishaps that occur in military engagements:

> The column was divided into two divisions; one part formed the main body of the column, consisting of H.M.'s 60th Rifles, 50 men; 86 men of H.M.'s 61st, 160 of the 1st European Bengal Fusiliers, 200 of the Sirmoor Battalion, 200 of the Guides' corps, 70 of the Punjaub Infantry, and 65 of the Kumaon Battalion, making a total of 831; the other part, called the support, consisted of the Jummoo troops, numbering 1,200 infantry and 200 cavalry, besides four guns.
>
> They all paraded at half past four on the morning of the day of the storm, on the Grand Trunk Road, opposite the Subzi-Mundi picquet. Every arrangement requiring Major Reid's supervision, and dependent on his foresight, was ready before the clock struck five. The only thing wanting was the artillery guns. They never made their appearance ... and when they did appear the officer in charge reported that he had only the proper complement for one gun.
>
> The day had more than dawned: it had advanced a little; and therefore none of our operations, so far as the light was concerned, could possibly be hidden from the enemy's watchful eye. The signal for Major Reid to commence proceedings was the loud crash which

64

was expected to ensue on the explosion at the Cashmere Gate. The Major, in breathless silence, was awaiting this sound. The Horse Artillery had not, in spite of the various delays, been equipped with the wanting gunners. Instead of the noise looked for in the neighbourhood of the Cashmere Gate, the reports of musketry shot struck on the ears of Major Reid. They seemed to come from the direction of his right. It was the Jummoo contingent, which had engaged the enemy; their act was premature, but there was now no help for it. Accordingly, Major Reid hurried, with sufficient force to the rescue, selecting the pucka road towards Kissengunge, as his way of advance.

Immediately, a skirmishing party, consisting of the 60th Rifles, was thrown out, under Captain D.D. Muter, on the right of the road; a 'feeling party' having preceded the entire column. The enemy had manned a breastwork which they had across the road, and another running parallel with the road. Both of these had been strengthened during the night. The enemy watched our advance, neither saying or doing anything until we were within fifty yards; they then saluted us most warmly with a well-directed volley. Being charged by the Rifles and Goorkhas, they evacuated their strong breastwork, and stood awhile in apparent perplexity, as to whether they should retire on the second breastwork or attack the Jummoo contingent.

Up to this time not a gun could be brought to bear on them, for want of gunners; otherwise, at this juncture, the enemy might have been mown down, like wheat beneath the reaper's sickle. Not only were we losing opportunity after opportunity, but the enemy were reinforcing their position at Kissen Gunge. And still more disastrous than all, just as Reid was about to make a feint on the rebel front and a real attack on their rear and flank, he was severely wounded in the head, and obliged to resign his command in favour of Captain Richard Lawrence; who had been previously in the secret of Major Reid's plan of attack.

This plan, I think richly deserves record. The position of the enemy at Kissen Gunge was formidable indeed, and the strength of the breastworks at the end of the road, already alluded to, was very great. No one was more alive to this fact than Major Reid himself. With anxious eye, during many a long and weary day just before the attack, he had watched the rebels, and seen them, sparing neither cost nor pains to give additional strength to that which before was very strong. He thought it was probable also that they might bring to their assistance, as soon as we advanced, light field pieces; which might play along and down the road by which our advance was to be made.

After having taken the breastwork across the road and close to the canal, it was the intention of the Major to have made a rush with half the column, to the angle of a serai in the immediate neighbourhood, and with the other half (whose first great duty would have been to get rid of some of the enemy who had lined certain garden walls which were in the vicinity) to march parallel to the first division of the column.

By this movement the breastworks at the end of the road would have been taken in front and in rear. The second or right division of the column would than necessarily have their right shoulders forward; and then the two divisions of the one column would have entered Kissen Gunge, simultaneously, at the breach made in the rear of the heavy batteries of the enemy.

After securing Kissen Gunge, Major Reid proposed turning the heavy guns, four in number (which, by the occupation of Kissen Gunge, he must have captured), besides two eight and a half inch mortars, which were also placed there, against the enemy in a place called Trevelyan Gunge. And if in addition to these six pieces of ordnance wrested from the foe, he could have combined with them the fire of those light pieces originally intended for him (and the want of them sadly hampered his operations from the very first) as well as the fire of the four guns in the Jummoo Contingent which were at the Eeeghur, the concentration of so much artillery upon Trevelyan Gunge would probably have led to its evacuation. And in the event of such a desirable contingency, leaving only some of the Jummoo troops within the serai, Major Reid would have proceeded with the remainder of his force along the dry bed of the canal, and so have entered the city by the Cabul Gate, which General Nicholson had promised to open for him.

Such was Major Reid's plan, which naturally enough depended much on circumstances for success ... But as providence would have it, another had succeeded to the command at the eleventh hour, and Kissen Gunge remained in the hands of the mutineers. The Rifles and Goorkhas in possession of the breastwork (which was taken gallantly at the charge, in which Captain McBarnett and Lieutenant Murray fell) continuing unsupported, were unable to maintain their position.

Nevertheless, Kissen Gunge was the scene of many an individual act of daring. The valour of Lieutenant Shebbeare, of the 60th Native Infantry, was very conspicuous throughout the operations of the day; and not less so was the conduct of Sergeant Dunleary, of the 1st Fusiliers, whose gallantry unfortunately cost him his life. Yet all was to no purpose. Our troops, particularly the Contingent, became completely disorganised. There was no rallying them. The Cashmere levies lost their four guns; themselves flying in utter dismay. And eventually the column fell back on its original position; not, perhaps, – despite its want of success – without having done some substantial service, in diverting the attention of the enemy from the main point of attack. But the losses incurred were something very severe.

From Captain D.D. Muter's letter of July 1858 to Robert Shebbeare, it would seem that Lawrence had responsibility for the much-maligned Cashmere contingent, while he, Muter, took charge of the withdrawal of the left column. His letter casts some interesting light on the matter of the behaviour of the Cashmere (Jummoo) contingent.

Norman did write to me about the Cashmere contingent, putting questions to be answered. I wrote to Dick [Lawrence] on receipt of the letter and asked him if he really meant to call in question the behaviour of such regiments as the 60th Rifles, the 1st Fusiliers, the Guides and the Goorkhas. This he disclaimed, at the same time that he maintained that the Cashmere contingent continued to hold a prominent position long after the European troops had been repulsed and driven from the ground. He also said that the contingent had not been defeated with the loss of their guns before we could come up, but that only a detachment of the force had been engaged (400), and that they continued to fight long after Reid was carried from the field, and that this occurred a mile from where we attacked. If this is true the Cashmere contingent as a body did not attack at all, for they most certainly did not support us.

Alluding to their occupying a position before this fortified serai, I observed in my answer to Norman that I considered it an erroneous charge against Captain Lawrence that he could have committed so gross a military blunder as to employ his men firing musketry at the walls of a position 10 feet thick. In attempting to carry such a position as that at Kissengunge I could only understand the attacking column going at the breach with fixed bayonets, failing to reform and go at it again, and finding it too strong and the loss too great to enable the place to be carried, to withdraw the column under fire and report the result to the authorities. I begged him not to get up a public controversy on the subject. If he does, I feel that he, Captain Lawrence, will not benefit by it. I see the beginning of such a controversy in the Lahore Chronicle where it is stated that the troops of the Maharajah had not justice done them in the despatches and a threat they would bring the whole thing up. I hate these controversies – they give rise to such a bitter spirit and leave the questions in more obscurity than ever. However, I am determined not to let the shadow of a slur to be thrown on any detachment of the Delhi Field Force that formed our column on that day, and I hope that the officers engaged will come forward and show that such an attempt will not be tolerated.

Major H.W. Norman, Deputy Adjutant of the Bengal Army, whose *A Narrative of the Campaign of the Delhi Army*[10] was the approved semi-official version of events, gives the following brief account of the actions that took place:

No. 4 column, under Major Reid, advanced from the Subzee Mundee towards Kissengunge, the Cashmere contingent co-operating on its right. The latter, however, was so sharply attacked by the insurgents, who were in great force, that, after losing a great number of men and four guns, they were completely defeated and fell back to camp.

Major Reid's column met with the most strenuous opposition, greatly increased, no doubt, by the failure of the Cashmere contingent; and the enemy were so numerous and so strongly posted, that after the loss of many men and officers, the Commander, Major Reid, having been carried away severely wounded, Captain Muter, 60th Rifles, the next senior officer, judiciously withdrew the troops to their former posts at Hindoo Rao's and in the Subzee Mundee. Their retirement was much aided by a fire of shrapnel shells, opened by Lieutenant J.A. Evans from the light guns at the battery called the Crow's Nest. One party of Guides Infantry, however, were surrounded in an enclosure, and could not get away. Their rescue was eventually effected in a spirited manner by the wing of the Belooch battalion, which, as before stated, had been detached to this quarter.

Brigadier Hope Grant's report of 17 September, adds some more detail:

A party consisting of an officer and eighty of the Infantry Guides came down to our support, and, though so small a number, went gallantly into the gardens and took up a position close to the battery. I regret, however, to say the officer in command, a most gallant young fellow, Lieutenant Bond, was wounded in the head and had to be carried away; but the Guides held out most bravely till they were

68

surrounded in the house and were in great danger; a detachment of the Beloch Battalion, under the command of Lieutenant-Colonel Farquhar, however, came to their assistance and brought them away in safety.[11]

Battles usually consist of a melange of small engagements and the descriptions above mention one in which Lieutenant Bond was involved. For the most detailed account of Robert Shebbeare's day we have his letter of 13 January 1858 (below) in which, with characteristic modesty, he devotes most space to a description of the death of his friend, Lieutenant A.W. Murray.

It is interesting that he gives no indication that the events at Kissengunge, for which he was awarded his Victoria Cross, were anything more than a normal day's fighting, but this is unsurprising, perhaps, when one considers that he had been involved in almost daily engagements with the enemy for three months. It seems likely that had the VC been awarded posthumously at that time, his great friend Lieutenant Murray, and Sergeant Dunleary, might also have received it.

Lahore, January 13th, 1858

My dear Father,

I have this day (my Birthday) received yours of 23rd November and as a mail has been advertised to close today, I hasten to give you what information I can about poor young Murray's death. He was with the Guides when I joined them, having been posted two or three days before. On the 23rd June we were ordered up from the right flank of the Hindoo Rao's position to support the troops engaged on the outskirts of the Subzee Mundee. We went upon extended order and on arriving near the houses the Guides went in with a rush and a shout, the pipes and drummers playing with all their might and dancing frantically. Murray and I were together then and his whole conduct then as on every other occasion before the enemy was most admirable. His courage and coolness fitted him perfectly for the management of the Guides, who are a very wild set and cannot be kept in hand without a good deal of tact and judgement and moreover have the greatest respect for any one who shows pluck and daring courage. On that occasion we drove the enemy out of the whole of their position on the Hindoo Rao's side of the Kurnaul Road and followed them across until we were recalled and ordered to confine ourselves to defending our own position and not to lose men by attacking them. I think it was as we were about to retire that poor young Murray received a bullet wound on the head, which however did not touch the skull tho' it laid him up for some time. I can't recollect whether it was the 9th or 10th of July [it was the 9th] that he and Bond were sent to hold the Sammy House (an old temple) which up to that time had not been strengthened in any way. The front wall of the yard even being broken down in many places and the gate only stopped up with branches. They held the place however with the greatest pluck, although completely surrounded at one time, and received the highest praise from Major Reid, Commandant at Hindoo Rao's, for their defence. We lost a great many men that day and Murray was hit at the back of the right hand by a bullet, which again put him on the sick list and eventually obliged him to go up to Simla on Medical Certificate. He recovered his health and came down to be in time for the siege.

On the 14th September we were with Reid's Column, the 4th, on the Kichengunge attack. Major Reid was shot in the head at the very commencement and the consequence was, that the Fusiliers, who led the attack, were not properly supported, as we in the rear had received no orders. However we, shortly afterwards, went up to the front and finding it impossible at the moment to advance in face of the terrible fire, from the front and flanking fire from both sides, we tried a garden wall which gave us some shelter. This position we held for some time. I tried to get the men to make another attack and jumped over the wall followed by Murray, McLean and Koodrutoola Subadar, with a sergeant called Dunleary of the 1st Fusiliers, two Riflemen and three or four Guides, but we were not supported and could do no good by advancing. I went back to call more men, while Murray with the others knelt behind a small bank. At this moment poor Murray was struck by a bullet in the middle of his chest and died in the spot. McLean said to him 'where are you hit?' and he put his hand on his chest but could not speak. His death was perfectly sudden. I did not know it at the time, for, seeing that the enemy annoyed our men very much by firing from a small temple to the right of our position, I went with some men to run them out. Shortly after we found the enemy coming round our flank to cut off our retreat and we withdrew towards our old position, as we could never have made good our attack on the guns in the face of the overwhelming force which had assembled against us. After we had retired I was grieved to find that poor Murray's body had not been brought away. Captain Daly, however, sent Koodrutoola with some men and they managed to bring it in next morning. I buried him at once and afterwards Captain Daly, Sir Edward Campbell and I went and read the burial service over his grave. Believe me, my dear father, your most affectionate son, Robert H. Shebbeare.

Later a tomb was put up in his honour with the inscription:

Sacred to the memory of A.W. Murray, Lieutenant in the 42nd NLI, and attached during the siege of Delhi to the Corps of Guides, who fell while encouraging his men to follow his own brave example on 14th September, 1857. In admiration of his unvarying gallantry, his comrades in the Guides erect this tomb.

Kaye gives a rather different account of Alexander Murray's death than that recorded by Robert Shebbeare in his letter.[12]

A party of the enemy sheltered by a breastwork were firing heavily upon our people, when some officers with a handful of men made a rush upon the work to take it. Foremost of these was young Murray of the Guides, who had been wounded in June and July, who had gone to the hills to recruit, and had returned to Delhi a few days before the assault. Speeding onwards with impulsive bravery, the grim message of death met him in the pride of his youth and the flush of his daring. He was shot through the chest and fell dead upon the field.

Most of the maps showing the salient features in the environs of Delhi at the time of the siege are rather general in nature, so of particular interest is Robert Shebbeare's own freehand diagram, showing details of the serai at Kissengunge, and indicating the direction of the enemy fire. From this, together with his letters, we get a first-hand account of what actually happened at the serai. (Notice that Robert Shebbeare calls it a mosque, rather than a serai.)

The official citation in the *London Gazette*, 21 October 1859, read:

Shebbeare, Brevet-Captain Robert Haydon. Date of Act of Bravery: 14th September, 1857 (India). For distinguished gallantry at the head of the Guides with the 4th column of assault at Delhi, on the 14th September, 1857, when after twice charging beneath the wall of the loopholed serai, it was found impossible, owing to the murderous fire, to attain the breach. Captain (then Lieutenant)

Shebbeare endeavoured to reorganize the men, but one-third of the Europeans having fallen, his efforts to do so failed. He then conducted the rearguard of the retreat across the canal most successfully. He was most miraculously preserved throughout the affair, but yet left the field with one bullet through his cheek and a bad scalp wound along the back of his head from another.

As one can see from the next letter, and several others, the carriage of correspondence was very unreliable and it would seem that a high proportion of letters and parcels went missing, so it is lucky that Robert Shebbeare duplicated some of the information about events at Delhi.

Camp Delhi, Lahore Gate. October 14, 1857

My dearest mother,

I am very much grieved to find from your letters that all mine have miscarried. By the first two mails after the Meerut Delhi outbreaks I sent five letters; three by the first mail by different routes and two by the second – By this means I thought I was making sure you would hear of my safety. Since then I have written a short note by every mail but one.

I had little time and less convenience for writing but I wrote each time to tell you that I was well and happy. You will also I fear have seen my name twice in the list of wounded, which would alarm you as you did not receive my letters.

I was wounded by three bullets on the 14th July and again by one on the 14th September but I am glad to say that I was not seriously hurt by any one of them. In addition to these wounds, two musket balls went through my hat; one while in the trenches at Hindoo Rao's and the other in Kichengunge on the 14th September. The first slightly grazed my scalp, giving me a severe headache and making me feel very sick. The second cut through a very thick turban and knocked me down on my face, but without doing me any injury. On the same day and shortly afterwards a ball hit me on the (right) jawbone but glanced off with no worse effect than making me bleed violently and giving me a very 'mumpish' appearance for some days.

I have indeed great reason to be thankful for my good fortune during the campaign. In the 1st place I joined the camp just at the right time; at the commencement of the business (it was not a siege until the 1st September) and was offered the post of 2nd in command of the Guide Corps, the finest regiment of Asiatics in India. This I of

72

course at once accepted, being very much honoured by the offer. Daly the Commandant took command of the cavalry and I held that of the infantry until the end of July when I got command of the whole corps, Daly having been wounded in action and my friend Hodson, who held the command after him, having raised a regiment of his own. From this time until the capture of the city I commanded the regiment. In the meantime, as I was only acting in the Guides, Hodson got me appointed 2nd in command of his cavalry regiment. So that in the event of the other officers rejoining the Guides I had that appointment to fall back on. Now, to crown my luck and satisfy me that I did not make a failure of my command in the Guides, I was recommended by General Chamberlain to Major Coke as 2nd in command, Major Coke being on the point of starting for England and the command of his Regiment remaining with me during his absence.

I write all this to you, dear mother, as it happened because you will understand that I write it for your satisfaction and to prove to you that I have not neglected my duty and that my conduct has been favourably viewed by my superiors; but I write in this style to no one but my Father and yourself and I sincerely hope that you will not show the letter to any one but our own family circle. Any one else reading it would put me down as a braggart, a character which I despise. I was hit oftener during the campaign than any other officer I think, but was always so little hurt that my friends used to laugh and say that I was made of India Rubber!

I shall remain with the Guides until some officer returns to take command of them and then I shall go over to Meerut and join Coke's Regiment. It is a rifle regiment composed principally of Pathans from the Peshawar district and Alfreedies, so I must begin the study of Pooshtoo (their language) at once. I have been fortunate as regards property, for I left almost all mine in Rohtuck, but I think the increased pay I have received has more than recompensed me and I may yet receive compensation from Government.

My future station will be Bunnoo or Koliat up near Peshawar I fancy; but it may be some time before the regiment goes back there.

I am going to send by this mail a coral necklace for Alice, or if coral is not fashionable as a necklace she will perhaps be able to make a bracelet of it. It is a piece of plunder from the city of Delhi though I did not 'loot' ie plunder it myself but obtained it by legitimate means. I hope Alice will like it and wear it for the sake of the brother she has never seen.

I have written a most horribly egotistical letter; but what can a soldier's letter be after a fight if not egotistical? I must close now but will write every mail.

With love to all, believe me dearest mother your most affectionate son

Robert H. Shebbeare

PS. Tell the girls that I have a great ugly beard and dress myself like a ruffian for want of a razor and good clothes.

Being wounded, Robert Shebbeare did not take part in the actions inside the city after its recapture, where a good deal of ill-feeling was displayed towards the inhabitants.

Indeed, the mutiny was a very bad-tempered and bloody affair and there are well-recorded accounts of many atrocities committed by both sides. From Robert Shebbeare's letters come little sense of the burning anger and desire to revenge the various massacres of British women and children that had taken place in the early stages of the revolt. This comes through from accounts given in many contemporary soldiers' correspondence, and these feelings were echoed in many sections of the press at home. Kendal Coghill, adjutant of the 2nd European Bengal Fusiliers, who went through the Cashmere Bastion at the storming of Delhi, writing on the 18th September, 1857, said, inter alia:

I had the satisfaction of receiving the 'King of Hindoostan' over as a prisoner and immediately placed him safe with a double sentry over him. I could not help calling him a pig and other opprobrious epithets and asking him about our families. I would have shot him dead if he had only looked up, the brute – and gave the sentries orders, if he tried to stir, to drop him. Captain Hodson and Lieutenant Macdowell of my regiment, attached to Native Sikh Cavalry, went in pursuit of the princes and overtook them about 8 miles off. Hodson had only 100 men and they had 10,000 men, but, thinking he was an advanced guard, they gave up their arms (the 3 princes, the Band of Christian Drummers of 28th N.I., and the English sergeant-major of the 28th N.I. who was formerly an artillery man, and during the siege pointed the enemy's guns on us, calling himself Sheikh Abdoolah and dressing like a sepoy). The band etc etc were killed on the spot but the 3 princes were brought with the sergeant-major to an open spot where the princes had commenced the slaughter and violation of our ladies themselves, and they were mercilessly killed and stripped and laid flat on the open ground till the dogs and jackals walked off with them. The sergeant-major is still in our Guard in irons and is going to be blown away from a gun in presence of the force.

Following the recapture of Delhi, Coghill went out to help clear the surrounding countryside.

4th October. 'Since writing the above I've been going all over the country as part of a flying column. Our column is 1,600 men, two 9 pounders and two 18 pounders pulled by elephants. The marching is awful as we march straight across country where there are no roads, and we drop by surprise in the night on villages and towns that befriended the enemy, and kept them in supplies, and cut up our ladies and officers when they were obliged to halt, at the first commencement of the outburst. Our cavalry surrounds the towns and we walk in, turn the women and children out, sack the place and fire it. Any that try to escape the flames get cut up. Sometimes by forced marching we manage to get two villages in a night – we have three columns out flying and revenging and you see the wholesome funk we have established over the country ... We are rapidly clearing the country up here, and sending into the Prize Agents any amount of plunder. Plundering for ourselves is not allowed, but as everyone does it, I have succeeded in boning two handsome Cashmere shawls value about £80 or £90 each ... take your pick when you get them and send the other to Lady North as a present from me for her kindness in getting me a position for life (and, I may say, a strong chance of death). Our Colonel (Showers) is Brigadier of this flying column: he has the pluck of the devil and his chief fun is dashing his own and other people's heads against stone walls.

As we have seen from his own letters, Robert Shebbeare's comments show no signs of the institutionalised contempt for the natives, and all things native, that seemed to have become endemic amongst the British. Indeed, his observations on the Indians with whom he came in contact are generally tinged with a mixture of affection, amusement and respect, and he seems always to be much concerned for their welfare. That such attitudes were not general can be seen from further comments made by Coghill in a letter to a sister dated 18 January 1858. His thoughts are quite representative of many writers at the time and it is possible that attitudes to native men were different amongst officers who served with European regiments, as did Coghill, from those who were in native ones, as were Seaton and Robert Shebbeare. At the outbreak of the Mutiny many commanding officers of the native regiments were incredulous at the idea that their own 'babes' and 'children' could possibly be plotting against them in their midst.

In case of accidents to the envelope, this is from K. Coghill, Adjutant, 2nd Bengal European Fusiliers, Delhi, to Mrs Tom Greene, Dublin:

My darling Silly, (a beautiful name for any one who will marry)

I have just returned from a wild goose chase in the district looking for that fabulous beast formerly known as the devoted Sepoy – but a pale-faced dog may now walk from one end of India to another, alone with a thick stick ... The niggers are the most cringing grovelling brutes conceivable – whenever they pass a European now they bow to the ground, and if an officer passes they keep their heads well down on the ground and feel thankful for a kick rather than otherwise, as it shows they have been noticed. Believe me, this war has been a first rate thing for the country – they used to be so cocky and thought themselves as good as Englishmen, but now it is all up with them for ever, and there won't be a chance of another war till we have to thrash the Sikhs who seem to think we can't do without them – whereas we had to waste all our good officers to mix with them to show them the way to the front.

In the same letter Coghill gives some insight into what happened at the recapture of Delhi, and on the subject of prize money, touched on in this book in the Introduction to Chapter Two, he waxes incandescent:

Is it not a howling shame that we have been done out of our prize money. The General distinctly ordered that he trusted Englishmen would remember their honour and country, and spare the women and children – to avoid plundering and looting, and that he would appoint prize agents and let the army select them, and when all the prize was collected, it should be served out equally to the troops with the sanction of the Queen, and now that stingy white Sepoy, Lord Canning (mutiny) has sent an order to say that the money is to be restored to the poor native who has been more wronged than he has wronged us. It's all very well for General Wilson to say he had his troops well in hand when he took the city, and so he had with one exception, which was that we were first told to kill every male in the place, which order we obeyed to perfection and were going on till the general came to the front and saw piles of dead and then he got soft-hearted and ordered the troops to desist from slaughtering. The only answer he got was a sort of silent growl that, 'now was the time for soldiers to do the work they had waited three months for and if they gave in then, before it was completed, the civilians would have the whole thing their own way, and let the cowardly rebels have another chance at our women,' and bang whack, they went on, the same as ever – every mussulman scoundrel was polished off till the General said the murder must cease and every native should be tried by military power, and then all hands quieted. The consequence is, not twenty men are hanged a day and there have come back into the city some 100,000 black brutes whom were the scum of Delhi, and the civilians say, 'poor fellows, they could not help it' … it is a shabby thing, to give a promise and then break it six months after it is given. Instead of prize money we are to have six months batta – which to a lieutenant is £70, whereas prize would be about £700, and to make it worse the niggers we ought to have killed are to get it instead of us – generosity!!!

These very selective excerpts have not been included gratuitously but are intended to show the kind of thinking prevalent among certain of the British at that time. Coghill, like many others, was obviously a man of 'strong opinions', which extend over a wide range of topics, and I include another just to show that anything was grist to the mill of these opinions.

I've always thought that it was all very well for men to travel and wander around the world looking for their bread and kicks, but when there are such glorious places as England and Ireland I don't think ladies have any right to roam in 'furrinn parts' amongst unwashed and uncombed foreigners.

He may be writing tongue in cheek, but then again, he may not! Letters from a different age reflect the beliefs of that age and in our more enlightened times today many of these will undoubtedly seem both incomprehensible and reprehensible to us. One should not attempt to make value judgements on what could only be described today as extreme political incorrectness. (Source: Coghill Papers, Centre for South Asian Studies, Cambridge University.)

Amongst the Shebbeare Papers is a pencilled note which reads:

To the officer commanding the Guides

The bridge to be repaired.

The Guides and guns to be placed on the bridgehead, having a support on this side.

A. Wilson, Major General[13]

This was the last piece of action in which Robert Shebbeare was engaged at Delhi, and although he does not mention it in his letters there is an account elsewhere.

On 20 September:

We took in succession the Lahore Gate etc ..., and now we hold the whole city. Every post is occupied save two, the bridge head across the Jumna and the Delhi Gate to the south of the city. To the former the Guides Infantry are about to proceed.' 'This was the last task entrusted to the Guides in the three months' siege. On arrival of the Infantry, under Lieutenants Shebbeare, Hawes and McLean, at the bridge of boats, it was found that the enemy had placed a 24 pounder gun, supported by infantry, on the opposite bank, so as completely to sweep the bridge. The Guides, however, charged across, where-upon the enemy fired a few musket shots, spiked the gun and fled; the Guides then brought in the gun.[14]

It is perhaps appropriate to end this chapter with words written long afterwards by Field Marshal Lord Roberts,[15] who said:

Where all behaved nobly it is difficult to particularise, but it will not, I hope be considered invidious if I especially mention the four corps most constantly engaged; the 60th Rifles, the Sirmoor battalion of Gurkhas, the Guides and the 1st Punjab Infantry. Placed in the very front of the position, they were incessantly under fire, and their losses in action testify to the nature of the services they performed.

Notes

1 An officer who served there, *History of the Siege of Delhi*, Adam and Charles Black, Edinburgh, 1861.
2 Revd. J.E.W. Rotton, *The Chaplain's Narrative of the Siege of Delhi*, Smith and Elder, London, 1858.

3 David, Saul, *The Indian Mutiny, 1857*, Viking, London, 2002, p. 150.

4 For a detailed account of this epic march, see McCrumm, Lieutenant General Sir George, *History of the Guides, 1846–1922*, Gale and Polden Ltd, Aldershot, 1938. During the many actions before Delhi between June and September Daly commanded the cavalry and Robert Shebbeare the infantry. He, Daly, rode into action in a velvet hunting cap. He later became a General and in 1869 was appointed Governor General's Agent for Central India. He left India in 1881 as General Sir Henry Daly and retired to the Isle of Wight to enjoy foxhunting. His *Memoirs of Sir Henry Dermot Daly* were published in 1905.

5 Hodson, G.H., Twelve Years of a Soldier's Life in India: Being Extracts from the Letters of the Late Major W.S.R. Hodson, London, 1859.

6 McCrumm, op. cit.

7 Reid, General Sir Charles, GCB, Extracts from letters and notes written down during the Siege of Delhi in 1857. Henry S. King, London. As Major Charles Reid, of the Sirmoor battalion of Gurkhas, he was in command of the picket at Hindoo Rao's House from June to September 1857, where he distinguished himself as an unflappable and very capable soldier. Had he not been wounded at the start of the assault on Kissengunge the outcome might have been different.

8 John Nicholson, perhaps the best-known and most controversial soldier of the period. A compulsive man of action with a superb eye for the salient points of a military situation, he arrived from the Punjab in command of a movable column set up to reinforce the Delhi forces. A constant thorn in the side of any superior officer whom he felt was not up to the job, he enjoyed an almost mythical status in the eyes of his Sikh troops, and his personal courage had been proved in many encounters in Afghanistan, the Punjab and Kashmir.

He left Delhi to engage the rebel forces under their commander-in-chief, Bakht Khan, who was on his way to intercept the British siege train being sent towards Delhi. It had been raining heavily, so the ground was a quagmire and progress very difficult, but he caught up with them at Najafgarh, beat them decisively and returned with thirteen out of the enemy's fifteen guns. He was mortally wounded during the storming of Delhi, and died some days later.

His story has been well documented and for a very readable account of his career, Hesketh Pearson's *The Hero of Delhi*, Penguin, London, 1939, can be recommended. It is quite likely that Robert Shebbeare may have met him, as Nicholson visited Major Reid frequently at Hindoo Rao's, during August and the early part of September.

9 Other sources mention that it was the Cabul Gate, and that General Nicholson would ensure that it was open by the time the 4th Column arrived.

10 Norman, Major H.W., *A Narrative of the Campaign of the Delhi Army*, W.H. Dalton, London, 1858. This was published in the *Overland Bombay Times*, from 23 January to 9 February 1858.

11 McCrumm, op. cit.

12 Kaye, Sir John, *History of the Sepoy War*, London (1867), in McCrumm, op. cit.

13 An artilleryman, Brigadier Archdale Wilson inherited command of the Delhi Field Force as a result of the deaths, in quick succession, of Anson, Reid and Barnard. William Russell, *The Times* correspondent, wrote in his diary from Cawnpore, in February 1858:

> I had almost forgotten, so very little is his presence remarked in camp, that Sir Archdale Wilson of Delhi is here in charge of the artillery ... he is rarely seen except in the evening, when he walks about with his cheroot in his mouth. I hear now, that much of the kudos he received was undeserved, and rather that it belonged to his subordinates. He is said to have been vacillating, undecided and desponding, and at the supreme moment he was overcome, and unable to give any orders – so Delhi men tell me. He is a tall soldierly man, with a small brow, quick eye, and large feeble mouth. But whatever his demerits or virtues, he was commander of the army before Delhi when the place fell, and his honours are due to him, and to his position.

His own letters to his wife confirm that he felt most insecure and out of his depth, but luckily several officers, particularly Nicholson, prodded him into taking decisions.

14 See 'Memoirs of Field Marshal Sir Henry Norman' in McCrumm, op. cit., p. 165.

15 From *41 Years in India*, the Memoirs of Field Marshal Lord Roberts of Kandahar, who had been Lieutenant Fred Roberts at Delhi, where he served on General Nicholson's staff.

Chapter Four

THE 15TH PUNJAB REGIMENT

It gives some idea of the responsibility that devolved to the relatively few British officers to note that Robert Shebbeare, while still holding the substantive rank of lieutenant, was sent off to the Punjab with orders to raise a regiment of 900 men from a motley collection of disparate men of differing religious and tribal affiliations, and it shows something of his character to find that in a short space of time they had become a well-respected soldiering unit. One can see from the photographs of the men that parade-ground protocol and elegant uniforms were not high on the list of priorities, though their demeanour is unmistakably warlike. The men were mainly recruited from low-class Muzbee Sikhs, and there was some anxiety expressed by the staff as to how they might conduct themselves. In the event, however, after a spell of general duties in the plains, in which they were engaged in pursuing rebels and dismantling fortifications, they were selected for duty as part of the expeditionary force sent to China where they acquitted themselves very well, and the letters which follow show Robert Shebbeare's initial lack of confidence turning to pride in how they had taken shape under his command. After the excitement of the events at Delhi it was perhaps fortuitous that the challenge of recruiting a new regiment presented itself so soon. It is apparent, nevertheless, that during his year in the Punjab, Robert Shebbeare suffered from the effects of frequent bouts of malaria which no doubt exacerbated an increasing degree of homesickness. After three months sick leave in Simla and a move with the regiment to the more benevolent climate of Oude, the tone of his letters becomes once again more cheerful and positive. During this time he would have been pleased to get letters from former colleagues and these have been inserted chronologically into this chapter.

Lahore Dawk Bungalow, November 1st, 1857

My dear Harry,

If my last letters, any of them, have been received at home you will probably be rather surprised at the heading of my letter. Indeed, I am rather astonished at finding myself in the Punjab so quickly. I had fully made up my mind to go across to Meerut to join Major Coke's Rifles when one day General Chamberlain sent for me and told me that I had been appointed commandant of the 15th Punjab Infantry and should start at once and cancel my arrangement with Coke; and I packed up my bundle, made over the command of the Guides to the next officer and started next day (23rd) by mail cart to Lahore. I was able to remain two days at Umballah and look after my property which I found all right – I packed what things I required and asked a friend to make them over to my servants who are coming up after me.

On arrival at Lahore I found that my regiment only existed on paper and that I had to raise it from the class of Muzbee Sikhs. They are the lowest class of Sikhs and the regiment is partly experimental. I must do my best for it and shall have much harder work than I should have had if the regiment were ready made to my hand. I am at present awfully uncomfortable as there is not one house vacant in Anarkullee where I have to live and I am therefore obliged to remain in the staging bungalow. I hope however to get some shelter for myself and my officers before long. The officers are, a 2nd in command, an adjutant and an officer doing duty – I have seen none of them yet but I hope to get a friend of my own to do duty, and if the 2nd in command and adjutant are good fellows we shall have a pleasant little mess I hope.

It is very uncertain where we may eventually be stationed but I suppose we shall not leave Lahore until the regiment is advancing towards its complement. The journey up was anything but pleasant. The mail is carried in a sort of dogcart built with much more attention to strength than ease and comfort. The horses generally gallop and the springs not being of the most flexible material the shaking and bumping are terrific even when the road is pretty good. 2nd November. I have just received Margaret's letter of September 8th. She asks about one Hill of the 60th. He is at Simla. He has been ill but is now well again, I believe. He was not a favourite of mine and I do not correspond with him so I can tell you no more. He was doing his duty with the Sappers and Miners at Delhi but went away on sick leave some time before the storming.

Colonel Seaton writes constantly but I will tell him what Margaret says. He is also at Simla. He was very badly wounded but is now nearly well. He has been out of all danger for a long time and suffers less pain than I did. Indeed, his wound has healed but the uniting of the muscles appears to give him a good deal of pain.

Innes is all jolly at Delhi and living with Grindall of the Commissariat in a nice house in the Chandnee Chowk, the principal street of Delhi.

Hay, a son of Mr Hay, of Hope's N.B. was very seriously wounded through the mouth at the assault. He is getting on famously and there is every chance of his recovering his power of speech entirely although it is at present rather damaged. His health is perfect.

Old Dickey Drought managed to get shot through the body and has become more of an idiot than before, I hear. He is recovering from his wound and will not eventually suffer from it.

Innes also got a slight wound in one of the first engagements but is, as I have told you, alright.

No other 60th officer was touched and all are at present alive* and as far as I know well so you may put an advertisement in the Times with all this information if you like but don't put my name to it.

No, *don't advertise*, but tell anyone you know. Some idiot did write a letter to the Times and wrought my name into it as you saw.

I stand five feet ten and three quarter inches and weigh 13 stone ten pounds but I am not *quite* a giant as the individual chose to call me, neither was I carried home. I remained with the regiment the whole day and came home with it.

I must close my letter and go and pay my respects to Sir John Lawrence.

With best love to all, believe me, yours affectionately,

Robert Shebbeare

*I think you mentioned having heard of poor Doyne's death from fever. It occurred at Umballah in August. I told you all about it in one of my letters. His wife is a wretch and cares little about his death except as far as it effects her pocket and comfort.

Anarkullee, Lahore January 13th, 1858

My dearest Nelly,

I have just seen an advertisement of a mail going out today and I can't miss the opportunity of writing to you on our birthday.

I received mother's letter of the 24th November today and was so happy to hear of your partial recovery from your terrible attack of sickness. I hope by next mail to hear of you being quite well and strong again.

I am living a tolerably dull sort of life just at present after all the excitement of the last few months. My regiment is gradually increasing and getting on in its discipline but I am afraid it will not be in a very efficient state for this campaign.

Lahore is very quiet and I don't know anybody but the officers of my own regiment. We have a game of cricket now and then but that is nearly our only amusement. Bye the bye, one of your friends the Bests is here, Henry, I think his name is. He is not quite as bad as his brothers, but still decidedly cracked. He received a wound in some of the cavalry affairs down by Allygurt, and seems to think now that he is entitled to the thanks of both houses of parliament if not Her Majesty in person! He is, like the rest of the interesting family, an intense bore and now that Mrs Best has written to him mentioning my name I shall never get rid of him! His brother, who was at Banda with me, I imagine from his way of talking of him, must be in a mad house, for which institution he was decidedly fit when he left Banda.

Could you not get some of your friends to do you in photograph again; I was unfortunate to lose the likenesses I had of you in camp at Rohtuck and am very anxious to possess others. I also regret to say that I lost on the same occasion the hair chain which was made in four pieces containing mother's hair, Margaret's, Emma's and yours and should very much like to have another if you could give it me. I have written my father such a long letter about poor young Murray that I am now pushed for time and must shut up.

Believe me my dearest Nelly, ever your loving brother

Robert H Shebbeare

I sent you a birthday present which you must accept with my best love although I could not manage that you receive it on the right day.

Futtygurh, 10th February, 1858

My dear Shebbeare,

Received the draft for R. 241.13.5, for which best thanks. I supposed there would have been some delay about your pay or that you would have sent the money sooner. I am in the same predicament and have been obliged to sell some things to carry on.

I am now in the Fort of Futtygurh and command the District which comprises Mynpoorie, Etawah, and Meerunka-serai and this place.

I am putting this fort into thorough repair and preparation for a siege which however I do not now hope will come off. The scoundrels, who are in some force are on the other side of the Raingunge, may cross and come and put themselves down on the opposite bank of the river and if they do I have got a nasty gun for them, a 32″ Howitzer, which will astonish their nerves. Hodson was severely wounded the other day across the right arm by a broad cut, but is all right and has gone in to Cawnpore.

Yours very sincerely,

T.Seaton.

Pray write to me occasionally.

The Chief's delay is all right. I know all his plans for he told me before he would make a fine finish of Lucknow and Oude.

P.S. Turner's Troop 9th Lancers, 1 EBF, HM 38th and 4th Punjab Infantry have crossed the river at Cawnpore and gone to Bonao. Frank's column consisting of HM 10th Punjab Infantry Regiment, eighteen field guns, two eighteen pounders and two mortars are at Budlupoor NW of Jaunpoor on the border of Oude. Culbee is taken in our hands and General Rose, moving up central India, must be at Jhansi.

Feb 14th, Murdan

My dear Sheb,

I have received yours of the 10th – herewith the Government Donation.

I am endeavouring to get your pay cleared up.

I am glad to hear so flourishing an account of your corps. I imagine the reason for the embodiment of the Muzbees to be other than any supposition of freedom from caste – a descent in the scale would hardly of itself procure that end. By combining in our view high caste and good soldiership we enormously strengthened the former, and by a general commingling we can get the soldiers without awarding all the fruits of our service and the pride of caste. We have taken a step in the right direction.

Some of the best deeds of soldiership in the Sikh Army were done by Muzbees and along the border the Guide work was proverbially good.

We have had a gorgeous k——— at Peshawar. Addresses and parades from a stout clearheaded soldier General Cotton. Speeches humorous and banquets rare for Edwardes. The men were truly pleased, though in the desire to attain a political end, the common sense treatment was rather overdone.

Kennedy has written to you. I asked him to mention Joree Sing to you. He says he can procure any number (to 200) good men for you. He is a gallant and good old soldier.

I shall be truly glad to hear you have promoted Ram Sing. I consider him as worthy of it as any man we have. Their pay shall be forwarded in a few days.

Should Government raise another Corps of Guides my voice would be heartily with you.

I was very glad to see your handwriting and though I have scribbled a scrawl amongst a heap of work try me once again and you shall be better treated.

HDD (Henry Daly)

Bond will make an excellent adjutant and can work now that the glory of war and fighting are over.

Camp Ackbur near Goozaira February 24th, 1858

Dearest Nelly,

This is the 3rd time I have commenced a letter to you this morning! I hope I shall succeed better this time than in the previous endeavours. The fact is that my moonshee (Persian writer) has been sitting on the floor close to me, reading the result of some very intricate accounts he has been engaged in for some days – but, as I don't care about them until they are quite finished, I tried to write letters while he read and explained, he thinking all the time, I fancy, that I was taking notes of his discourse. He was so voluble, however, that although I know nothing of his accounts I utterly failed in my letters. He is off now, I am happy to say, and I may succeed in making myself intelligible.

I did not receive your Christmas Day letter until after those of January had arrived, which delay prevented my first learning the news of your recovery from your own handwriting – I hope dear Nelly that ere this your health is fully reestablished and that you are as strong as ever. I did not forget you on our birthday and I hope that you will have received the little present I sent you by Mr Jones of the 9th Lancers. I can't tell what can have become of Allie's necklace. If she does not receive it I must send her another. I sent it by post, but the post has been very uncertain since the outbreak.

I hope you will see a great friend and favourite of mine before long, C. McLean of the 1st Cavalry. He is about the best Highlander I ever met and a brave and spirited young soldier, and I am sure you will all like him. Pray tell Jack to give me the benefit of his foreign experience in France, which language I can still read and understand very well, although from want of practice rather doubt my pronunciation.

I shall be so glad when I can learn anything about what is likely to be the fate of our service. I am afraid we shall not benefit by the transfer of authority to Her Majesty's Government. I can form no plan in my furlough until something is settled. I received the photograph of grandmother which Margaretta sent me and it strikes me as being rather a good one. I wish you could send me your own likeness; I lost all I had at Rohtuck.

We have been expecting an account of the commencement of the siege of Lucknow. I hear it was commenced on the 23rd. If it did you will hear of it from the newspapers.

There is the moonshee again! I find I have no chance of escaping this time so I must cut short my letter, although I really think I have nothing more to say.

Your ever affectionate brother Robert H. Shebbeare

Goozaira. April 20th, 1858

My dear Nelly,

I was delighted to hear by the last mail of your better health and that you were well enough to write me a note yourself. I am afraid the weather must have been very unfavourable to your recovery, but I hope by this time it has been sufficiently warm for you to get a change of air. We are at last under a roof again – not before it was desirable though, for the heat in tents had begun to be very great and would have done us no good after our last year's exposure.

We don't seem to be getting on much in India, whether the fault lies with Lord Canning or Sir Colin Campbell. I wish with all my heart that the home Government could be induced to try Sir John Lawrence as a governor general. In common times Lord Canning might be well enough, but now we want a tried man and one well acquainted with the people of the country – and Sir John is the man. But I fancy his chance is small as he belongs to the Company's service and is therefore looked upon with jealousy by the noblemen who are at the head of Her Majesty's Government.

I shall be very glad when the India Bill is settled and passed. There seems to be no chance for our old Master John Company. I wish he could have lasted my time for I despair of getting a better.

We never see a fresh face out at this vile place and therefore have no news except from your newspapers and letters. I am glad my friend McLean has been appointed Adjutant of his Regiment so that he will have something to come back to when his leave is up. He has gone I fancy to England but I know nothing about him, as he has never written one word since he left us. I hope nevertheless that he will look you up as I desired him to do. I can't complain about people not writing to me; but I did expect to hear from McLean and when you see him I hope you will tell him so.

Will you please tell Harry that I have heard of the pistol. It has been started from Kurrachee and I expect it Goozaira shortly. I am so glad that Jack has got this appointment and that he has escaped the necessity of going to Edinburgh. Fancy living among Scotchmen for three years! I hope he will write to me and tell me about the business and how he likes it, what he has to do etc. Oh dear! I wish I could come home and see you all! I hope things will be so settled before the end of next year (at all events) that I may be able to do so. I was in hopes of getting mail from home before closing this but I can wait no longer although the mail will probably be in tomorrow.

With best love to all, believe me dear Nelly, your most affectionate Robert H. Shebbeare

30th April. To give you an idea of the dress of my regiment I send you scraps of stuff showing the colours of coat and turban, khakee coat and chocolate turban.

This sort of animal. They never shave nor cut their hair but tie the latter up as you do your 'hack hair' but they put it on the top of their heads.

Here he is without his turban. Pencil very bad.

Goozaira. June 8th, 1858.

My dear Mother,

I received your letter with Margaret's of the 2nd May a day or two ago and I must confess my negligence with regard to answering questions so I will first proceed to answer all those I find in your last three letters.

Young George Baker has got through all the fighting safely and considering that he is not very strong at any time his health has been wonderful. His name is George Anthony Aufrere Baker, his father a naval officer residing at Leamington. I should not be at all surprised to find that he is related to Mrs Aufrere for it has always appeared to me that he was in some way related to or connected with every second person I met. This country at all events is full of his uncles and cousins; Plowdens, Hardinges, Hunts, Stewards, Ansons and Youngs, amongst others, and his numerous cousins have always been a matter for jokes in the old regiment. I will ask him the question however. I have never seen or heard from Colonel Riddell since the outbreak, but I see by the papers that he commands a column, of which his regiment (3rd European Bengal Regiment) forms a part, in the Mynpoorie and Etawali country and is doing well. I am sorry he did not get any earlier opportunity as he is a first-rate officer and very energetic. Colonel Seaton was never permanently attached to the 60th. He was sent temporarily to take command from Colonel Drought who was rapidly ruining the Regiment. Sir Thomas is now to go to Shahjehanpore, a very important position where he is likely to have work until the country is cleared of the ruffians who are hanging about in bands.

H. Arbuthnot I have never met. I am afraid Captain Jones (he was promoted without purchase for good service) must be suffering from his wounds or he would have delivered my parcels before this. I think Harry might well have asked him for them. By the by it is possible enough that he went home quickly and left his baggage and this would account for the delay. I have never heard from young McLean since he left Goozaira. If he does not pay you a visit I hope that Harry or Jack will use violence if they can find him and force him to call on you and give an account of Goozaira at any rate.

I have heard nothing of Mr Innes since I left Delhi but I saw his name in orders for leave so I suppose you will see him soon. He will be able to find McLean who took a box home for Mrs Innes. The barbarian himself will probably be off to the Highlands before long but he ought to present himself to you as early as possible. I am very much obliged to Harry for getting Margaret and Helen's likenesses taken for me and it will give me great pleasure to receive them.

I wish I could get pictures of my Father and yourself and indeed of the whole family.

There does not seem much chance of any legislation with regard to India for a long time. Lord Palmerston and Mr D'Israeli are very amusing on the subject but after three months Parliament appears to be no nearer a decision. The amount of nonsense talked and the absurd mistakes made, in both Houses, on Indian subjects, are ridiculous in the extreme. What will become of us eventually it is impossible to guess.

Please tell Harry how glad I was to receive the 'Illustrated Times' and 'Courier de l'Europe'. The picture of poor Hodson in the former, though somewhat like, would give a stranger no idea of him. He is represented with a sort of rough beard which he never wore (at least not habitually). His hair was of the very lightest flaxen whereas the print gives the idea of dark brown or black. But I must close my letter.

Hoping it will find you all well,

with best love

believe me dearest mother, your affectionate son

Robert H. Shebbeare

Palace Delhi, June 14th, 1858

My dear Shebbeare,

Very many thanks for your kind congratulations.

I should like to have seen your name amongst the Brevet Majors; had you been a Captain you most assuredly would have got it. It is a great pity you were not.

I shall have very great difficulty in replacing all the little fellows. Jang has put his veto against recruiting. The guards at the different ghats are more vigilant than ever. Soorbea sent a man into Nepaul the other day to try and get some fellows to join. He has done so at once, and forced Jang's service! I hope to get away from this vile hole before the end of the month. Certain it is I must go. The head bothers me a great deal and the medics say I ought to be in the hills. I came back to my work too soon.

You have done well to get your regiment completed so soon. You deserve great credit.

The account of poor Murray's auction was made over to Hawes before he left this, and the money realized was sent him with a guard some time ago. He acknowledged the receipt of the draft and said he would make the sum over to you. Apply for your brevet majority on promotion. I shall be happy to testify to your conduct on all occasions and will give you all the assistance I can.

Believe me, yours very sincerely, Charles Reid

I have not heard any Lucknow news today. Yesterday Hodson has been reported dead and Taylor wounded. All was going on well. Delhi still stands. 'A standing disgrace to the nation', I call it.

We shall have a row with Ranee. Let me get a thousand Goorkhas together . . .

Letter from D.D. Muter, 60th Rifles, who commanded the 4th column after Major Reid was wounded on 14th September:

Allahabad, 4th July, 1858

My dear Shebbeare,

I received your letter of the 7th July with much pleasure. Many thanks for your kind congratulations. I doubt much however about the lieutenant-colonelcy. I would have the most wonderful luck if I got it considering what I have done and comparing it for instance with what you have done.

I look upon you with very great admiration – I say this without any flattery. In fact I can neither write nor talk except as I think. I say I classed you as a man who can look death steadily in the face and accept it in preference to a shade of dishonour. Now, it is all very fine talking, but among those of a very high standard of spirit you will not find this self devotion, it is only in the very highest order, and I rank you in that order and respect you accordingly – now these are not empty words which I say to you. I will if necessary say to the Horse Guards and will most certainly do so if you are not immediately promoted, on obtaining your company, to the brevet rank. It would come better from me than any remonstrance from yourself. I would certainly consider it a slur on all at Kissengunge if such services that you performed on that day were overlooked though I regard it as quite an absurdity to suppose that you, who commanded the Guides, should be passed over – the thing is quite impossible. I allude as far as I am concerned only to the act of one day. If you like to go in for a Victoria Cross for your gallantry in leading over the garden wall and the devoted attempt you made to reform the troops for a third attack on the serai of Kissengunge, I am your man. As you say it is absurd to suppose that there are not men as deserving who acted in the great event that redeemed India (Delhi was India saved) as in the common military operation against Lucknow, and certainly you are no common claim. You see that the fluke of my having been for a short time in command of the column at Kissengunge gave me the power of bringing your name up and this I am not only willing but anxious to do, satisfied that nothing in the way of reward that could come of it would exceed what you deserve. Write on the subject if you wish the stone to be set rolling. Nothing may come of it, but something may but at any rate your name will be up before the authorities. If I write, should the application go through Chamberlain who commanded on the heights or straight to the C-in-C or to England to Wilson? It is because no one has been pushed forward that so little has been got for Delhi. If the divells won't move, let us try our hand, we can only get snubbed.

Norman did write to me about the Cashmere contingent, putting questions to be answered. I wrote to Dick [Lawrence] on receipt of the letter and asked him if he really meant to call in question the behaviour of such regiments as the 60th Rifles, the 1st Fusiliers, the Guides and the Goorkhas. This he disclaimed at the same time that he maintained that the Cashmere contingent continued to hold a prominent position long after the European troops had been repulsed and driven from the ground. He also said that the contingent had not been defeated with the loss of their guns before we could come up, but that only a detachment of the force had been engaged (400) and that they continued to fight long after Reid was carried from the field, and that this occurred a mile from where we attacked. If this is true the Cashmere contingent as a body did not attack at all, for they most certainly did not support us.

Alluding to their occupying a position before this fortified serai, I observed in my answer to Norman that I considered it an erroneous charge against Captain Lawrence that he could have committed so gross a military blunder as to employ his men firing musketry at the walls of a position 10 feet thick. In attempting to carry such a position as that at Kissengunge I could only understand the attacking column going at the breach with fixed bayonets, failing to reform and go at it again, and finding it too strong and the loss too great to enable the place to be carried, to withdraw the column under fire and report the result to the authorities. I begged him not to get up a public controversy on the subject. If he does, I feel that he, Captain Lawrence, will not benefit by it. I see the beginning of such a controversy in the Lahore Chronicle where it is stated that the troops of the Maharajah had not justice done them in the despatches and a threat they would bring the whole thing up. I hate these controversies – they give rise to such a bitter spirit and leave the questions in more obscurity than ever. However, I am determined not to let the shadow of a slur to be thrown on any detachment of the Delhi Field Force that formed our column on that day, and I hope that the officers engaged will come forward and show that such an attempt will not be tolerated.

I have luckily got a good house though up so late in the season. Brougham's mountain train went down and he vacated this and was glad to get a tenant for the other half of the season so I only pay half the rent. Hawes is near this and another young fellow of the Guides. Hawes rides with Mrs Mundy every evening – the place is pretty full and pretty dull, nothing going on. Edwardes and Chamberlain are here. They are supposed to be busy answering questions about the native army and its organisation. If you come up here remember that I have a little room at your disposal. This is the high road to Cashmere and I propose to pay that unhappy valley a visit in the autumn. What say you, have you ever been this pilgrimage? In case it is necessary before you go home our spare room is not the sort of place that one would ask you to in the plains, but here the case is very different. They say the climate after the rains is magnificent and the scenery is certainly very grand and beautiful.

I suppose I will soon hear from you on some subjects that I have broached. I have often intended writing to ask you if any notice had been taken of the strong terms in which I mentioned you in the despatch I wrote for Kissengunge for it is very unfair that the only officer who was selected out of many that behaved so well and in such a trying affair and on so grand an occasion should be passed over in silence, and it surely can't be a reason that my insignificance should be an excuse for not rewarding your gallantry.

Sincerely yours, D.D. Muter

Murree, 10th July '58

My dear Shebbeare,

I am happy to tell you that I have ascertained you were amongst the subalterns recommended for reward in the list sent by Sir A. Wilson which was supported by Sir C. Campbell. As a subaltern I expect you can get nothing but I hope that on obtaining your captaincy you will be at once promoted. R. Lawrence is harping on the old strain and writes upon the laudable and valuable service of his contingent. They may have done a great deal, but I cannot find any one to say so who did not belong to them. Like most forces of native allies I take them to have been a nuisance but I do not wish to say so publicly and hope I shall not be obliged to do so.

Yours sincerely,

H.W. Norman

Norman, Henry Wylie (1826–1904) entered the Indian army at the age of seventeen. He went through the second Sikh campaign and having attracted the favourable notice of Sir Colin Campbell, was selected by him to accompany an expedition against the Afridis in 1850 as officiating brigade major. He served in numerous frontier expeditions between 1850 and 1854, and in the suppression of the Sonthal rebellion of 1855–6. In the Mutiny campaign he was constantly engaged, being present at the siege of Delhi, the relief of Lucknow and a number of other affairs. As assistant deputy adjutant-general of the Delhi Field Force, he was one of the leading spirits of the siege, and afterwards became its chief chronicler. Altogether he was mentioned twenty-five times in despatches. He afterwards became assistant military secretary for Indian affairs at the Horse Guards, military secretary to the government of India, military member of the Viceroy's Council and member of the Secretary of State for India's Council. He had a distinguished career as a colonial governor and in 1893 he was offered the viceroyalty of India, but, after first accepting, declined it. In 1902 he was made a field marshal. He died in 1904. (*Memoirs of Field Marshal Sir Henry Wylie Norman*, 1908)

Goozaira, July 20th, 1858

My dear Mother,

By Harry's letter received this morning I am sorry to find that you had received no letter from me for two mails. I have only missed one mail since I have been at Goozaira so I don't understand this. It is rather difficult when letters are posted from this place: as sometimes it is safe to send them by the quickest route via Agra and Indore and sometimes not, so one of my letters may have been late. There is a rumour today that it is the 'latest safe day via Mooltan' so I write although I believe that three days hence would be soon enough.

Everything is pretty quiet in India just now. The rains have set in all over the country and prevent the movement of troops. What arrangements will be made after their cessation I cannot guess. I hope we will be able to get down to join some part of the Army, but I think it is doubtful. However, they may want pioneers and then we must go.

The dullness of this station in the hot weather is scarcely to be described and in the cold weather it is disagreeable enough although one can find amusement in shooting. If, as I hear, our Delhi prize money is likely to turn out well, my prospects of paying you a visit as soon as furlough is opened is very much improved. I can't take more than six months leave to England without giving up my appointment and under common circumstances I should hesitate to spend the large sum of money which my passage to and fro would cost on a six month trip, but if we get good prize money I shall not care about doing so. I should only have four months in England, a short enough holiday after fifteen years of regimental duty in India! but I got my staff employ through luck in being in Delhi at the right time, and not through any interest, and it is very possible that if I gave it up I might never get another. However, furlough will scarcely be open for a year and we cannot tell what may 'turn up' in that time. Harry is kind enough to send me Punch and The Times occasionally. I have been very thankful for them but we have now arranged a sort of club and take Punch, the Illustrated News and the Evening Mail ourselves. To add to the other horrors of Goozaira our beer has now run out and we can get no more at present, a lively prospect for the rest of the hot weather! How dreadfully slow the proceedings of parliament on the India Question are! I am afraid we may linger on in suspense for the next five years. I suppose the Government 'dodges' it to get through the session safely. It is quite impossible not to laugh at the nonsense talked on the subject by people who know nothing about it. Mr Layard is the laughing stock of India! I must close now,

Believe me dear mother, your ever affectionate son

Robert H. Shebbeare

In the autumn of 1858 Robert Shebbeare went on sick leave to Simla, suffering from the persistent fever and headaches he had noted before and which were eventually to kill him in China; from the note below one can assume that he was being treated for malaria, of which there are several forms.

Statement of the case of Lieutenant R.H. Shebbeare, commanding 15th Punjab, age 31 years.

Temperament. Sanguineous

Habits. Temperate

Period of service. 14 and a half years

Leave of absence. None.

Lt. Shebbeare was exposed during the whole hot season of 1857 in the operations against Delhi, and suffered at frequent intervals from severe fever accompanied with head symptoms. In October last year he was ordered to Lahore where he remained until January. Whilst there he had little or no fever, but on being ordered to Goozaira and remaining exposed in tents until the end of May, fever returned and he continued to have constant and severe attacks until the beginning of August, when at the recommendation of his medical officer he obtained 60 days privilege leave and proceeded to Simla.

For a considerable time after his arrival here, in fact until the beginning of the present month, the fever attacks were of frequent occurrence and he had gained nothing by the change. It was then checked for about a fortnight but, I regret to say, has again returned and within the last ten days he has had four severe attacks, one of which was more severe than usual.

I do not consider him now at all free from it nor do I under the above circumstances consider him in a fit condition to proceed to the plains, and therefore I would advise his getting an extension of one month for the purpose of getting as much change as possible by marching about in the hills.

The treatment has been that usually adopted in such cases, large doses of quinine, aperients etc.

Signed A.C.C. De Renzey, assistant surgeon in joint charge, Simla.

Professor Nicholas Burgess, formerly of the Royal Defence Medical College, London, has kindly supplied the following note:

From what you said, I am fairly certain that the problem was caused by malaria, the type caused by Plasmodium vivax which was very common in India and SE Asia at that time.

Typical symptoms are as follows: after an incubation period of a week to several months from the time of being bitten by a female anapholes mosquito, there is an abrupt onset of cold chills and shivering (usually starting about midday to early afternoon and lasting about an hour), followed by fever, headache, nausea, vomiting and abdominal pain (lasting 4–6 hours), and then drenching sweats for 1–2 hours as the temperature falls. Relapses may occur weeks or months later in treated cases, but at regular intervals of three days in untreated cases. Common long term effects are enlargement of the spleen and sometimes its fatal rupture, and acute liver failure. (See also Robert Shebbeare's letter of 10th August, 1860.)

Quinine has been used in the treatment of malaria for hundreds of years, long before anyone knew what caused the disease. The relationship between the causative organism and the mosquito was only confirmed at the end of the 19th century. There are annually still over 4 million deaths worldwide from the disease.

Camp Nawabgunge,

On the road between Cawnpore and Lucknow. November 17th, 1858

My dear Harry,

I have just heard that we must write today to be in time for the mail, so here goes just to let you know what I am doing. We marched from

Cawnpore on the 18th and were stopped here by an order from Lucknow. There is a rebel called Benee Madho about the country here who can't be caught. I say 'about the country' advisedly for we hear of him twenty-nine miles to the south one day and ten miles to the north the next and sometimes he is reported in two places at once, so we get knocked about a good deal and catch nothing. The C-in-C is somewhere close at hand and also a column under Colonel Eveleigh, but Benee has given them all the slip, and is now reported to be away towards Baraitch. The fact is it is difficult to get information about him as the people are friendly to him and he can of course spread false reports as to his whereabouts with great ease. I should like to catch the beast! What may become of us if Colonel Eveleigh's column returns, as seems probable, I can't say. There will be more troops here than are required so some of us will move off I suppose, but in what direction it is impossible to say.

I have no news for you and am up to my elbows in monthly returns, muster rolls etc. so can't write more.

Believe me, yours affectionately

Robert H. Shebbeare

To Henry F. Shebbeare 5, New Square, Lincoln's Inn, London

Camp near Lucknow, January, 30th, 1859

My dear Harry,

I write this on the paper you were kind enough to send me. It is very jolly, and I am thankful for it. I am very much disgusted to find by my mother's letter of December 16th that some of my letters have miscarried. I hope that they have reached you ere this, at any rate you ought to have received my letters from Cawnpore and Nawabgunge. I think I wrote from Lucknow last month but I am not certain.

Since the 13th December we have been out with a column under Major Maynard, H.M. 88th. This column was broken up on the 20th January and since that I have been moving about the country collecting arms and knocking down fortifications. I have special magisterial powers from Mr Montgomery and have a lot of other work to do so do not find much leisure time. It is a beautiful country, perfectly flat and the crops splendid. The forts were chiefly built of mud surrounded by belts of impenetrable bamboo, and through jungle. It is very hard labour getting rid of the latter. I think we shall go into Lucknow in a few days as they want native troops there and we are able to remain there during the hot weather. I am so well now that I see no chance of getting home on medical certificate in the autumn as I had hoped to do, but one must not complain of good health. I don't see much chance of getting into a house in the hot weather; we shall probably be obliged to build ourselves some sort of sheds and get through the heat the best way we can. I am very much afraid Mr Murray has never received the box I despatched for him. It is very disgusting; I suppose it has gone the same way as Jones's baggage! I have written all the way down the Mooltan road to agents and merchants but can hear nothing of it as yet. I received a letter from him (dated July) in December. He could not have received it then but I took no notice of the date of the letter at first and wrote off to the agents from whom I can hear nothing. I got a letter from him (the son) dated May on the 8th or 10th of January! What can one do with the posts and roads in such a state? I heartily wish I had had nothing to do with poor Murray's estate. The bother I had with the accounts was bad enough, and I am out of pocket by their being confused during the first part of our stay in Delhi. All the officers who made purchase at the auction were scattered about and some have been killed and others are in England so I had to pay for them as they should have paid cash, but there was no cash in those days. However I had rather pay the whole than Mr Murray should lose the box. I hope in a few days to know about it however one way or other.

Goodbye, with love to all at home, believe me,

yours ever affectionately,

Robert H. Shebbeare

Camp Mahomedabad, about 25 miles from Lucknow. February 29th, 1859

My dear Nelly,

I begin scribbling now so as to have something ready for the mail which ought to leave for Lucknow in a few days. We seldom hear when it is to start until the days before and then there is no time to write comfortably, for if I know that I am obliged to write at a fixed time, it becomes an irksome duty instead of a pleasure.

I have been wandering about this part of the country ever since the 13th December and it is still very pleasant, although the warm weather is coming on apace. I think I shall be recalled to Lucknow in a few days as I wrote to the Secretary to the Chief Commissioner telling him I had finished all the work laid down for me. It is a beautiful country, probably the most fertile part of Oude, as level as a billiard table with immense groves of mango trees and most beautiful crops which are now ripening rapidly. The country people are as civil as they can be and are, I believe, really glad to have come under our rule again, always excepting a few of the most powerful of the large landowners who cannot make so much money by oppression as in the time of the Kings.

I am glad George Baker went to see you, he is really a good lad and a good brave soldier. If you see him again tell him that the horse I bought from him died a month ago, a loss of £80 to me. The worst of it is that depending upon him for my parade work I had sold a very fine young Arab who would have made an excellent charger and am now left in the lurch for horses are difficult to get and the price enormous just now. It is all very fine for Messers Innes and Baker to tell you that I can get fifteen months leave without losing my appointment, they don't seem to tell you that a medical certificate is necessary to this arrangement. If I get one I shall make a start of course, but at present my health is so alarmingly good that the prospect is poor of getting three doctors to say that it is indispensable that I should go to England! I hope that you won't apply again to Captain Jones (as mother threatens) for those parcels. He will send them directly he gets his baggage, I'm sure. I am exactly in the same position with regard to poor Murray's things. I sent them off in July or the beginning of August and they have never reached. I write about them constantly but can find out nothing about them yet. There is a fatality attending all letters connected with the affair too, I believe. A letter from Mr Murray dated July reached me in November. A letter from his son the ADC dated Lucknow, May 1858 reached me in January 1859 and a letter I wrote to him a month ago has probably carried as I can get no answer. I hope the box may turn up shortly, but I can do no more than I have done.

The Government has just sanctioned the establishment of a band in the regiment. I have had one 'on my own hook' a long time, but now we get 100 rupees a month and the musicians are paid by the Government, so we shall get on. I have been able to pick up some tolerable musicians and with my old men from the 60ths we make a pretty good noise! When we get in to Lucknow I hope to get one of the bandmasters of the regiment there to look after my boys twice a week or so.

Harris writes me word that the Delhi Photographs have arrived, so I shall despatch them directly I get in. You will like them very much I think (if they ever reach you!). Am I not writing nicely today? I generally flatter myself that my writing is rather neat, but I have hurt my hand and the pen won't go straight.

I am glad you all like Hodson's letters. I have written for them and hope to have them in a few days. I met him first at Umballah and we were very intimate. His wife is gone home. I don't much like her. She is clever but vulgar and Hodson would have got on much better without her influence. She was very fond of him and that is about all the good I can say for her. I met young Arbuthnot of the 4th Cavalry the other day but had only just time to speak to him. He seems to have a pretty good opinion of himself: but is a gentlemanly, nice-looking lad. Tell Jack I will cultivate his acquaintance when I return to Lucknow.

I have made quite a collection of native arms, swords, matchlocks etc since I have been out. I shall send a few of the best home if possible. I can't hear anything of Mrs Peskett for the last two months. I get no answers to my letters and don't know where she is. They were to have paid a visit to Cooksons at Meerut in December or January but I don't know whether it came off or not. I have been anxious to hear as the poor little boy was very ill when Mrs Peskett last wrote. The cook has just come in to say that he is roasting the sirloin but is unable to give us any horse artillery with it! It is supposed that he means horse-radish. There – now I have a letter ready to send whenever I receive notice of the 'latest safe day'. Anything more I may find to say must go in a postscript.

Believe me dearest Nelly,

your ever affectionate

Robert H. Shebbeare

PS I am in grief about the shirt collars! Will you ask Jack to send me a pattern of the 'collar of the period'. I like those that turn over if their day is not past, as my beard don't agree with all rounders if very stiff!

Camp near Lucknow, March 14th, 1859

My dear Mother,

I am afraid you have never received one of my letters in which I asked you to address to Lucknow. I shall get them a week earlier than if sent to Lahore. You may now address me as captain for my fifteen years service gives me the brevet rank. Of my regimental promotion I see no chance for a long time.

15th. I began this letter yesterday morning but was attacked by such a violent headache that I could not continue to write but was obliged to darken the tent and lie down all day. I am not quite rid of it even now, so must confine myself to telling you that I have been in good health and am so still but for this headache which I am liable to get at any time. I must send this into Lucknow by a camel rider or it will not be in time for the post which leaves today.

Hoping this will find you all well and happy,

I am, dear mother,

ever your affectionate son,

Robert H. Shebbeare

P.S. I have got the Delhi photographs and shall despatch them directly I go into Lucknow; also some ferns for Nelly collected at Simla and Mussoorie.

Lucknow, September 5th, 1859

My dear Mother,

After a long interval I received today your letter of the 24th July. It was more than two since I got a letter from home and I had begun to be anxious. I have not behaved myself well in the matter of writing letters, some of which you seem not to have received. I cannot tell you how it is but the post seems to be very irregular now, I have no doubt that I shall eventually get some letters from you which I ought to receive before that which came today, but what can be the reason for this irregularity I cannot guess. Some of our newspapers come straight to us but others of the previous month afterwards.

I have really had nothing to tell you since I came to Lucknow. I have been doing nothing but the routine of regimental work. I am living in a good house on the banks of a nice river. I go out very little, indeed I may say not at all. I have few acquaintances and no friends except those officers who live with me, Randall my 2nd in command and Harris my adjutant. For the last few days we have been digging for some treasure supposed to be concealed in the house but at present without success. There may be treasure however, and if so we should get a 4th share so I hope we may hit on it yet. Jack Hayes's retirement makes me a captain and I believe a major by brevet.

Colonel Norman wrote to me the other day that Lord Clyde has recommended me for the Victoria Cross so I shall get it before long. I told you that I thought I should get it but you did not seem to think it likely and Harry said he would believe it when he saw it in the

102

Gazette. I should not have said anything about it if I had not thought and been told that it was pretty certain. You will now see that I was not far wrong.

I don't know what to say about taking my furlough. I believe I can only get it by giving up my appointment and as I like the regiment and have not the chance of getting another after coming out I don't like to give it up. Believe me I think all day and dream all night of that happy day when I shall see you all again. I hope it will arrive and that soon. I am in too good health to extract a medical certificate although I am really very much broken and have little of the strength for which I was formerly rather famous. I must wait for 'something to turn up' like Micawber.

There is talk of some Sikhs going to China but it said that Lord Canning with his usual imbecility has refused to send any troops without orders from England. I hope that if any Sikhs go my regiment may have the luck to be included and I have the men well in hand and feel they would do well.

6th. G. Arbuthnot is to spend the day with me tomorrow. He has done so several times of late but otherwise we see little of one another as he lives in the old cantonments about four miles from our house across country and some seven miles by road. He was hoping to get home with the discharged Europeans but was too junior. He is looking well and reading the languages pretty steadily I believe. I did not much like him at first as he had a self-sufficient manner but this has been rubbed off and he is a general favourite now. I like him very much and should see more of him were we not so far apart.

About the European disturbance, you ask what I think of it. I believe that although it is difficult to say whether the men had a legal right to their discharge, yet as the sum would not have been very large the Government might have been liberal and have given the bounty. If this had been done no agitation would have taken place and scarcely a man would have thought of wishing for his discharge, whereas now hundreds of men jumped at the chance of getting to England although almost every man of them will enlist again before six months are over.

7th. Arbuthnot is here puzzling over a Hindoostani exercise with Harris my adjutant. He is getting on and I hope he may pass, more especially as the examination is likely to be very easy next month. An order has been issued that every officer shall be removed from staff employ unless he passes in November. There are so many unpassed officers on staff employ that unless a great proportion of them pass the public service will come to grief. Therefore it is supposed that the standard for examination will be lowered.

15th. I have not found anything to say although I commenced this letter on the 8th. The mail goes tomorrow. I send you two copies of a picture which was taken the other day. Randall is on my right and Harris on my left and the dog 'Loot' in the fore ground.

Believe me dear mother,

your affectionate son

Robert H. Shebbeare

Lucknow, October 1st, 1859

My dear Mother,

Here we are waiting the arrival of the Governor-General, Commander-in-Chief and all the Bigwigs of the land who who are to hold grand court at Lucknow about the 15th of this month. During their state we shall I fancy never be out of our war paint. Lord Canning is travelling on this progress in a much more magnificent style than any of his predecessors have done for years and as we have all lately been taxed to make good the deficiency in the Indian finances you may imagine there is no little outcry against him in consequence. I wish he would be recalled, as he seems to be getting more and more imbecile. General Grant at first ordered my regiment down to the new cantonments to take part in the sham fights which are to take place, but at a hint from me that my men were sufficiently worked already with the city duties and that we were remarkably well off where we were, he kindly countermanded the move and says we may stop in our present quarters for a year more if the C in C does not interfere.

Again we have always a chance of being turned out by the Civil Authorities as the house may very probably be given back to its former owner. However I hope this will not be the case.

No chance of our going to China. I think that no native troops will be sent. Never mind, I am comfortable and well off here. Mr Phelps the Parson of the Parish says he married a daughter of Mr Hughes Hughes who is a friend of my father. I only heard of it the other day in a note I had from him on business, and I have not called on him yet as he lives some six miles from us, but I am going to do so. I wish however I knew something about Mr Hughes Hughes. I recollect Mr Hughes of Ryde, one of whose daughters married

Urmiston but I don't recollect that he rejoiced in that duplicated name? Will you tell me all about them? I am writing with ink which seems to act as printer's ink and I am afraid my note will be hardly legible.

Believe me dearest mother,

with kindest love to my father and all at home,

ever your affectionate son

Robert H. Shebbeare

Chapter Five

CHINA 1860

The two China Wars of 1839–42 and 1856–60, also known as the Opium Wars, were the results of threats to the trade in opium established by the British during the first part of the nineteenth century. Under the aegis of the Honourable East India Company, opium was grown in India and exported (smuggled) to Canton in China, where it was disseminated widely via a black market network. Income came both from taxes on the Indian growers and from the sale of the opium, the proceeds of which were invested in tea for export to Europe. By 1839, there were an estimated 2,000,000 addicts in China and the Emperor appointed Commissioner Lin to bring this widespread addiction under control. After Lin took strong measures amongst the local population and destroyed several thousand tons of opium that had newly arrived from India, the British sent a punitive expedition which took a number of Chinese cities and annexed the island of Hong Kong. Under the Treaty of Nanjing (1842) the Chinese were forced to pay a huge indemnity and to open five ports for trade; during the next few years trade agreements were extended to other countries as well as Britain. War broke out again in 1856 when the Chinese made an allegedly illegal search of a British ship, the *Arrow*, and the British and French went in with warships again, resulting in the Treaty of Tiajin (1858), whereby the Chinese had to open further ports to allow Christian missionaries to practise in the country and to legalize the import of opium. Attempts by the Emperor to prevent diplomats entering Peking were seen as an excuse to enforce European authority, and the British and French mounted an expedition which culminated in the sacking of the Emperor's Summer Palace in Peking, thus effectively ending all further resistance.

Lucknow, January 10th, 1860

My dear Mother,

I have had very sad news from you of late. Your letters tell me of the loss of poor Aunt Fanny my Godmother and now I hear from Arbuthnot that Jack is laid up with the smallpox. Arbuthnot got letters by a later mail than mine and I have heard nothing of Jack from you. I am now anxiously looking out for letters.

I told you some time back that I wished to go to China. Well, I'm going. The regiment was asked to volunteer and has done so and I am expecting orders to be off very shortly. It is the best thing that could have happened for me and opens a much better prospect of visiting England. General Grant commands and his present staff with all of whom I am intimate accompanies him, so we shall go under very favourable circumstances. I can't say when we may start; I was at the General's at breakfast this morning and he could not tell me anything about it. The whole business seems to have been so badly managed in this country that I really believe Lord Clyde himself does not know who is going. I have so much to do that I have not one moment to myself. I am writing from morning to night until I get quite stupid over it. I will write at more length when I know more of my movements. I really am very anxious for your next letters.

With very best love to all, believe me, my dear mother,

your affectionate son,

Robert H. Shebbeare

On 1 February 1860, Robert Shebbeare bought a copy of *Letts Diary and Almanack* in Lucknow, in which he kept occasional notes about regimental matters. Following the orders to join the China Expedition, there was a rush of small daily entries, of which the following is a sample:

4th Feb. Completed the numbers of the regiment. Could have enlisted a very large number from the police, chiefly mussulmen.

5th Feb. Sent off the first batch (thirty-seven) of women and children to Lahore, and a very difficult business it proved. At first I could get none of them to start and then they all wanted to start at once.

11th Feb. Marched from Lucknow to Buntera – Left Nuttha Sing to send off the remainder of the women [some relief, no doubt!]

15th Feb. Harris with 1st detachment of 300 men started for Allahabad by rail.

16th Feb. Officers posted in General Orders, 19th Feb

Lieutenant B.H. Smith, late 67th
Lieutenant F.E. Sotheby, 2nd BRB
Lieutenant H.D. Metcalfe, late 25th NI
Lieutenant W.G. Keppel, 6th Europeans
Lieutenant E.B. Ward, late 48th
Lieutenant K.M. Pratt, late 51st
Lieutenant J.F. Elton, late 37th

After several days marching they arrived at Raniganj

24th Feb. Had breakfast at the worst hotel in the world and went on by rail (to Calcutta) with Chalmers and Major Synge, 43rd. Found Wolseley and Spencer and dined at Wilsons with the China Staff.

In Calcutta, Robert Shebbeare was engaged in trying to sort out logistical and supply problems of various kinds and making purchases on his own account.

25th Feb. Breakfasted with Lumsden. Reported to Becher. Gave orders for clothes to Harman and Co. The 19th Punjab Infantry still in the river as the Marine department cannot supply tugs. 2 or 3 cases of cholera recurred and they were landed somewhere down the river. Went to Cooks and looked at some horses. Ordered boots at Saxton and Walkers.

27th Feb. Simpson required indents for:- Blankets, 1 each man, Canvas frocks 2 each man, 10 mounds Ghee, 10 mounds Borax. Bought saddle and holsters and ordered four Nolan's Bridles at Cuthbertson and Harpers.

29th Feb. Went with Lumsden and Allgood to two bullock train companies to try and get the regiment brought down. Neither of them could do it.

2nd March. Telegraphed to Randall for Nuttha Sing and 3 men; also told him to hurry on. Lumsden telegraphed about the elephant.

3rd March. Parbuttee Churn Nundun is to make me 12 degs of copper with cover and spoon to be ready by 15th March. Bought 12 yds. Blue serge at 1.4.0. per yd. for servants.

6th March. Ordered 12 more degs with covers large enough for the former degs to fit into. And also 12 large plates 3 feet in diameter. [Large indeed – perhaps these were for the cookhouse.]

Calcutta, March 13th, 1860

My dear Nelly,

I received your short note of the 25th January only yesterday after I had sent off a letter to Harry and I fear that the mail has gone out. However, this will probably reach only a week later.

I am exceedingly glad that you received the ferns in good order for I thought they would never return from Lincolnshire! I gathered them all myself while in the hills with the Pesketts. The photographs are very good and cost a good round sum of money so I am glad you got them although I might have replaced them. The ferns I could not easily have got again as I am not likely to see the hills again for some years.

You are quite right in all you say about India; it is quite intolerable to me now, much as I liked it before the mutinies. Everything is changed and in my opinion for the worse. I would gladly give up the service if I had enough to live on at home. I had hoped and wished to get home this year, but it is right that I should see service and as I and my regiment were selected I am really glad to go. I have a great deal of anxiety just at starting but when we once get rid of the pilot and see blue water I shall be very happy. It is really quite a comfort to think that at last I am about to leave this wretched country even for a short time. I hope to get away home directly the business is over, and I don't think it will last very long. If I had had the luck to get my majority this China business ought to have made me a lieutenant colonel, but I must not growl but be content with getting for China what I ought (as everybody says) to have received for Delhi. I think a good growl does one good, and occasionally indulge in one accordingly, but it does not last long.

My dear Nelly, you say that you would almost agree to come to India to see those ferns in their natural state. Allow me to assure you that nothing, not even the beautiful scenery of the hills and their delightful climate, could compensate for one tenth part of the discomfort and the dreariness of the life in the plains and few people are lucky enough to be able to remain long in the Hills. My dear girl,

I would not have you, or any one of you, come out here on any account. Oh!! how I do dislike the sight of the yellow white faces of the ladies of Calcutta and what a treat it is to see a fresh arrival from England. Even an up country face is pleasant to look on after the dreadful corpse-like countenances of Calcutta.

I wish I could find out where Mrs Peskett is. I wrote and asked them to come over to Lucknow for a day or two on their way to England and have never had a line since and although she had written just before that they were going home by Calcutta, I can hear nothing of them. Both Peskett and herself were ill and I have been anxious to hear. Do you know anything about them?

I think I told Harry in my last note to direct to Hong Kong for the future. Hong Kong! It sounds more outlandish than Goozaira. I shall not finish my letter today but will add to it from time to time. 1st April. And I am not off yet; however, I hope to start on Tuesday and I shall indeed be happy to be off. Two ship loads of my men have gone off already and I go with the rest in the 'Bentinck', an old overland steamer (now bought by the government) and we ought to be very comfortable. G. Baker comes with me to China and sends his love: I applied to head quarters for him and he was at once appointed. Will you please tell my father that Grindlay's people still send the home news to Goozaira. Hong Kong will be best for the present.

I am going to send home to Harry a box of favourite swords and other curious arms, I want him to get them from Grindlay as early as possible and open the case, otherwise they may get spoilt and I should be very sorry to lose some of them. I am also sending a box containing clay figures very well executed of some of my men etc, which will give you a very good idea of the men and uniform. The poor old tailor! He had been in my service for upwards of fifteen years and died in Calcutta directly he arrived. I regret him immensely. He has always been an honest and faithful servant. You will see a likeness of him in the box which I think very good. F. Innes will certainly recognise it. I am writing in such a terrible hurry and in a room so crowded that I must beg you, dear Nell, to overlook any obscure passages you may meet with in my epistle as I have not time to read it. Bye the bye I will enclose a copy of verses which you may understand; I cannot.

Now with love to all believe me

ever yours most affectionately,

Robert H. Shebbeare

(The clay figures mentioned were commissioned by Robert Shebbeare and have an inscription 'Gopaul Dass fecit'. They were given to the Sandhurst Museum, which is now part of the National Army Museum.)

Lines addressed to Captain Shebbeare's Corps under orders for China, 27 January 1860:

Go forth ye sons of Mahood Of Brahmin and of Ram,
By bravery gain glory To your tribes in Hindustan
And o'er the children of the sun May your right arms prevail,
From the river banks of Peiho To the walls of far Canton,
Stay not the tide of battle Till the victory be won.

'Victoria' be your motto, Your Empress and your Queen,
Go fight beneath her banners, Let your loyalty be seen.
For by your deeds in that far land, Ye warriors rest assured,
Ye will be judged by nations, Let a good name be secured.
Then neath Britannia's standards If ye find a bloody grave,
Your names shall be recorded, And deathless, dying brave.

Calcutta, 16 March 1860. Extract of a letter to Miss E.M. Shebbeare:

I have been here since 24th of last month, having been ordered down by dawk to make arrangements for the China business. My regiment arrived at Ranigunj yesterday and is to come here on the 18th or 19th by rail. You will easily understand that it is a very anxious time for me. Sikhs as well as all other natives of India look with dread on the voyage and the sojourn in foreign countries and though I think my men are cheerful and jolly, yet I have constantly to think of and carry out innumerable little plans to increase their comfort and prevent their regretting that they have volunteered. General Sir Robert Napier has command of the embarkation and does everything he possibly can to make the men comfortable. I shall be very glad when we are off. Cholera is flying about and both Fane's and Probyn's are losing men.

Robert Shebbeare sailed from Calcutta on 15 April and his diary records that in his cabin aboard he had with him:

111

Contents of No. 1 Bullock Trunk

Posteens and furs, Chocolate pugries, Undress belt, Black Inverness napper [presumably a cape], Books, Flannel shirts, One pair lace boots, Light summer waistcoats, Hair Oil in case, Khaki trowsers.

Contents of No. 2 Trunk, to be in cabin

Full dress uniform with cummerbund, Mufti coats and trowsers, Medals, Warm socks, coloured and white, Black coat, Flannel shirts, White shirts, Towels, Stud box, Pyjamas, Pocket handkerchiefs, Citrate of magnesia, Khaki coat, Wide Awake [a type of hat].

Valise, in Cabin, Toilette apparatus and 1 change, Memo books.

Ship Bentinck, Hong Kong. 21st May, 1860

My dear Mother,

Here we are safe and happy after a very pleasant passage. We shall go on I believe in about three days and then I shall have more to tell you than I have now. The mail is in today but I am obliged to post this without waiting for the distribution. Innes was here at dinner yesterday looking very well. I received your letter through the Admiralty immediately on arrival here.

I dined with Sir Hope Grant the day before yesterday and he was very kind and made a great many enquiries about the men. He has had to leave two Sikh regiments behind but he would not hear of our regiment being left. I am as usual in a hurry having left my writing to the last moment, but I did not like the mail to go without a line or two.

With best love to all,

believe my dear mother,

ever your affectionate son,

Robert H. Shebbeare

Hong Kong, June 1st, 1860

My dear Harry,

I sent you from Calcutta 'By long sea' two largish boxes, one containing clay figures of my men etc., which will perhaps interest you, and the other containing a number of swords and curious arms. The figures will receive no damage I hope, but I fear the swords will be very rusty. There is one sword called 'misnee' which I have worn constantly but which is now done up elaborately in a red velvet scabbard with gold mountings. I should be very sorry if this were spoilt as it is a present from Nuttha Sing. By the present mails (Steamer Madras) I have sent a box full of silver ornaments, bracelets etc. It is addressed to Alice under cover to Grindlay. I enclose today a bill for £10 on the Oriental Bank which I hope will cover any expense which you may be put to on account of these packages. I hope that Alice will be able to select something from the box which may console her for the loss of her coral necklace which was lost and that she will serve out the other articles to her sisters. I forget what is in the box exactly so I can give no list.

We ought to be off north this evening but it appears inclined to be squally and it is very possible we may stop another day. Tell F. Innes that his brother is looking well and happy; he goes north also. Will you go to Grindlays as soon after receipt of this as you can and pay for Alice's parcel? It rains almost all day here and there is no fun of any kind going on. I shall be very glad to be off. Continue to direct to 'China Force, Hong Kong'.

Believe me yours ever affectionately,

Robert H. Shebbeare, Captain

I am so bothered with public letters that I have signed myself 'Captain' from force of habit.

On arrival in Hong Kong two entries in the diary note:

May 15th. Called on C-in-C and Lady Grant. Dined with Wilmot; Sotheby with me. Got a terrible ducking as it rained cats and dogs. Borrowed clothes from Col. Bruce and Wilmot and turned out in most gorgeous staff war paint.

May 16th. Dined with the Commander-in-Chief. Saw Fane's beautiful scrapbook and heard excellent music. C-in-C on violincello.

Deep Bay, Hong Kong Island, Steamer Bentinck

June 3rd, 1860

My dear Jack,

We left Hong Kong on Friday and went out to sea about two hours before dark, with the 'Queen of the East' and 'Pioneer' in tow; about ten o'clock the wind rose and by twelve it was blowing a gale and there was a very heavy sea on. The 'Pioneer' carried away both her hawsers a little after midnight and went off on her own hook. We held on until daybreak when we went round and made for Deep Bay which we reached safely with the 'Queen of the East' in tow. We could hear nothing of the 'Pioneer', but found that three other steamers which went out at the same time as us, had cast off their ships and come in. In Deep Bay we found the 'Viscount Canning' which started two days before us with Randall's party. In the evening the Admiral came round in a small steamer and ordered us round the island to fetch the 'Pioneer' which had come in about four miles off. We went round and anchored by her for the night and brought her into Deep Bay this morning. There are some five and twenty vessels lying here, all waiting for fairer weather. The wind is still from the NE, a very unusual quarter at this time of the year as the SW Monsoon generally sets in about the 10th May. HM Transport Steamer 'Assistance' ran on to a reef which is marked on the charts, in broad daylight, and is now a complete wreck. She had 800 China coolies on board and a few European soldiers. I fancy all were saved but have not heard anything certain. The wreck is within 300 yards of the shore and is above water forward. There are ninety-one hired transports that I know of taken up for troops to the north and I don't know how many government vessels besides. I think John Chinaman will begin to look about him when he sees them sail into the Gulf of Pechili! Some China men in Canton offered to bet 20,000 dollars that we shall be licked in the North. They were taken up by the joint stock company of officers, chiefly staff, I hear. The French ran a ship on shore also the other day in the same stupid manner as the 'Assistance' and I hear that they have lost all their artillery harness!

Young Keppel of my regiment told me the other day that he has an uncle or cousin living at Surbiton who knows you but I cannot recollect the name. If you know who he is you can tell him K. is quite well and jolly. He is on board the 'Viscount Canning'. Innes is at anchor within a few yards of us and I mean to go and see him when I can get hold of a boat. Baker is on board with me and very jolly.

Saturday was a day to be recollected by our Sikhs. They have been so accustomed to fine weather and smooth seas that they were quite taken aback and did not know what to make of the heavy sea which tossed us about in every direction. I suppose the ship we were towing had some effect on our own motion for we pitched and rolled and kicked and jumped in a most extraordinary way and for the first time during the voyage I was most woefully and unmistakably sea-sick and was very glad when we ran into smooth water and anchored in Deep Bay.

114

The regiment arrived at Singapore on the 27th April, having experienced a dead calm the whole way, which was lucky for the steam transports as they were towing one, and sometimes two sailing vessels. There was very little sickness amongst the men and they were all very happy and in good spirits. [Extract of a letter from Lt R.H. Shebbeare to his home, by kind permission of his niece Miss M.L. Shebbeare.]

His diary tells us that the *Bentinck* anchored in Talien Bay on 17 June, in heavy fog, and one of the men had his leg broken by the hawser. On the 18th he called on General Sir Robert Napier and the following day on General Mitchell. At 5.30 am on the 20th, 100 men under Elton went ashore to build a jetty and to dig for water, returning at 4 pm. Entries tail off and the last, on 30th June, records that 'Nuttha Sing found some pennyroyal. Thermometer 86 degrees at 11 am in bell tent.'

Camp Talien Hwan in Manchooria. July 10th, 1860

My dear Nelly,

We are still here waiting for the French who will probably not be ready for the next fortnight. They are encamped at Cheefoo on the opposite side of the Gulf of Pecheli so I cannot tell how they are getting on; but I know we have had to supply them with powder, artillery, harness and a great number of other things which they had either lost by allowing their ships to go on shore or else had never brought at all. I wish we were independent of them as we are losing the most valuable part of the year through their not being ready. Lord Elgin arrived yesterday in the 'Feroze' so I suppose their preparations will be hurried on. I don't know whether Baron Gros is here or at Ceefoo (I don't know the spelling). I hear that Sir Hope Grant is gone over there today.

We were sent on shore on the 25th and at first were rather badly off; but we have now found our mess tent and some preserved meats, soups etc., and everybody tells us we are much better off than any other regiment. We have brought some of our Indian experience of camp life and I find that we manage better than the English regiments. We get very bad fresh beef but no sheep at all. My knowledge of cooking comes in usefully and I am generally asked to make a stew or some dish more savoury than our cook treats us to. The commissariat bread is scarcely eatable and we get very few vegetables and the Bay appears to have no fish. We bought a six-oared gig from the captain of the 'Bentinck' and row about the

115

harbour a good deal. My horses I am glad to say arrived in very good order and the new charger is turning out pretty well. I fortunately brought leather water bags and a pack saddle so the pony makes himself useful, the water being rather scarce and the wells distant. My men have dug some ten wells near our own camp but there is very little water in them. I am sorry to hear this morning that Brigadier Crofton, commanding the artillery division, is ill. He hurt his leg while getting out of a boat and neglected to take proper care of himself; he is said to be seriously ill. I hear of no other officers in bad health and as far as I know the troops are healthy but we have only one division of infantry on this side of the Bay. The 2nd division of infantry and the whole of the artillery and cavalry are on the north side about nine miles off, where the water supply is better.

There is a curious and I think rather disreputable old fellow here called Maturin or Matchurin or some similar name out here who says he knows my Father and he was certainly aware that his chambers were in 5, New Square. I suppose he must be in some way acquainted with him. Nobody in the whole army seems to know what he is and it is impossible to get him to tell. He told me that he was two years with the Duke of Wellington and that he came out here in the 'Odin' with Lord John Hay, the Duchess's brother, but Lord John tells me that he himself does not know who or what the man is. He says that he was also in Canada with Lord Elgin and in fact he has apparently been all over the world with all sorts of noblemen, but whether as secretary or valet-de-chambre or in some other capacity superior or inferior no one can even guess. The general supposition is that he is a newspaper correspondent but he calls himself, or rather leads other people to call him Captain and hints that he is attached to the Embassy. In short he is a perfect mystery and although he is generally partially intoxicated he is quite impenetrable. The climate here is very good really at this time of year. Thermometer about eighty degrees in mess tent at 2 or 3 pm and sixty-four at night. We have brigade parades three times a week and rather more than our usual allowance of working parties, pickets etc., but not enough to fatigue the men. I think General Mitchell and Brigadier Sutton are as good and pleasant commanders as we could have had and both seem to be very pleased with the regiment. I hope they may think the same after seeing it in action and I think they will not be disappointed.

Signor Beato the photographer is here in the village close by. He wants to take my portrait he says, for his volume of Indian celebrities! so I am going down in all my war paint this afternoon or tomorrow.

We have made up a code of signals and are now asking the 'Bentinck' to send off the oars of our boats which have been sent on board for repairs. The signals will I hope be useful to us through the campaign.

In case I should get a chance of sacking a town what particular article of Chinese furniture or apparel would you like me to steal for you? The villages about here are almost entirely deserted and the Provost Martial people are very active so that it is almost impossible to get even a cabbage or an onion. My soldier servant Dyal Sing does sometimes manage to get me a few eggs and occasionally a fowl, but then he is a remarkably clever fellow and has the command of a large bag of cash or Chinese halfpence which I brought up from Hong Kong.

The mail goes out on the 13th and I shall not close my letter until the evening of the 12th. My old friend Heathcote of the Rifles is now here with the 2nd Battalion and I am glad to be near him again. Colonel Palmer who commands the 2nd Battalion and Captain Bowles were also in the 1st Battalion at Delhi, and there is a brother of Sir Edward Campbell's also here; but I am afraid this battalion will not in any way be equal to the first as it is almost entirely composed of recruits. (In explanation of the cause of all my blots and scratches let me tell you that some twelve subalterns are clamouring for tiffin in the mess tent where I am writing).

I got my Mother's letter of the 24th April through the Admiralty and I am very delighted that you can occasionally write in that way as the post is so very uncertain and I have had no Post Office letters since I left India. Bye the bye, I must not forget to send you a copy of an epitaph on a tombstone in the graveyard in 'Happy Valley' at Hong Kong. I think it is the most exquisite specimen of that style of composition that I have met with.

12th. I have been ordered on a court of enquiry at ten o'clock and must therefore close my letter. A marine who was servant to Lieutenant Hudson commanding the Gunboat 'Leven' took up a pistol and shot his master through the neck the day before yesterday. After firing the shot he went on deck and told the Master that Hudson wanted him. The Master went down into the cabin and the Marine fired at him through the skylight, hitting him behind the ear. The ball lodged in his arm. Hudson is dying but the Master is out of danger. I must now positively close with best love to all,

Believe me, dear Nelly, ever your affectionate brother,

Robert H. Shebbeare

In his memoirs, Harris notes:

On landing at this place I saw, with great pleasure, that the whole coast was covered with oysters – real natives. I at once sent back a message to the chief engineer ... asking him to send me a bucket and an oyster-knife. Later on I got a hammer and a chisel, and next morning the beach was a sight with 8,000 men eating oysters ... Two days afterwards one had to walk for miles before finding an oyster.

We stayed at Ta-lien-whan for about five weeks. The climate was glorious, the scenery beautiful, and the food excellent. We had no sickness, and during the whole campaign I do not believe we had more than three men at a time in the hospital. Truly, the China campaign of 1860 was the most enjoyable picnic in which I have ever taken part.

Gulf of Pecheli, Ship Bentinck. 10th August, 1860

My dear mother,

I am just recovering from a severe attack of fever and liver which commenced on the 26th, the day we left Talien Bay. I am in hopes that the liver is reduced to its natural size again now and I feel no pain in it so that I may be said to be quite well, but I have not got a bit of strength in my body, my legs are ridiculous to look at and I can hardly lift a cup of tea. Now however the mutton chops commence and I hope a glass of beer and I trust I shall pick up rapidly. Meantime my regiment is on shore under Randall and although it could not be in better hands, yet I can't help regretting that I cannot command it myself. The regiment is gone out today to take some entrenched camps [the Taku Forts]. I hope most sincerely to join in about five days more. I am very comfortable aboard the 'Bentinck'. The captain has made me up a large bed in the saloon and sends Lascars to pull my punkah all night. He has indeed been most kind to me all through my sickness.

I will write to you by the next opportunity and hope to have more cheerful news.

Believe me

dearest mother,

your most affectionate son,

Robert H. Shebbeare

The note below was attached to the end of the letter by Miss Helen Shebbeare, his sister:

But they were unfortunate in losing their first Commandant Captain R.H. Shebbeare, VC, who was at this juncture taken ill after the capture of the Taku Forts, as the following orders show.

Headquarters, Camp Sinho, 15th August, 1860.

Leave of absence upon the recommendation of a Medical Board is granted to Captain Shebbeare Commanding 15th Regiment Punjab Infantry, to proceed to England for 15 months under the new regulations. By order Fred Stephenson, D.A. General

This was the last letter that he wrote and for the poignant details of his attempts to join his regiment, and of his last illness before he embarked for England, we must rely on a letter from his great friend George Baker. In a later letter of condolence written to Charles John Shebbeare, Robert's father, he describes how he had to be carried back to the coast and taken aboard the *Emeu*, bound for England.

It was indeed most pathetic that, having at last got his first home leave, he was to die at sea off Shanghai so shortly afterwards; and it was all the more a harrowing tale in that his family, including the sister to whom he had written and sent gifts, and one of whom he had never seen, were waiting expectantly for his long-anticipated arrival home. We can only imagine the awful sense of shock and loss that they must have felt at the dockside at Tilbury on being told the news of his death, and it is difficult, indeed, not to share in a little of their grief ourselves.

To Charles John Shebbeare

15th Punjab Infantry Regiment, Camp Hong Kong, December 30th, 1860

Dear Sir,

On our return from the north of China the most distressing intelligence of the death of your son reached us while on the homeward journey and plunged us all into deep sorrow. At the hazard of reopening your grief I take the liberty of addressing you, as well as expressing my own deep sympathy in your bereavement and to give you a melancholy account of his illness north and departure for England, as doubtless it will be satisfactory to you and Mrs Shebbeare to know he was well nursed, that every care was taken and that I only left him when he was comfortable aboard the steamer.

From the day he left Calcutta your son's health began to fail and he was greatly troubled with sickness and faintness early in the mornings but at Talien Bay he became much better and joined us in long walks in the mountains. Just before we left he again began to suffer and before we had arrived off Pehtang he was forced to report sick. The liver being much inflamed it was thought necessary to apply leeches but though we searched the fleet thoroughly not one had survived the journey north.

The regiment landed, leaving him on board the 'Bentinck' under the care of Dr Meyer the ship's surgeon, an able man, and Captain Hodge, who was kindness itself. Unfortunately your son suffered greatly mentally. His gallant spirit chafed at being left behind. He had determined to lead the men he had raised and to be lying down weak and ill when all were up and doing affected him most seriously. His whole mind was centred on the Regiment and when the heavy guns were heard on board his excitement was intense.

Finally, on learning the date on which the assault was to take place, he determined to land and take command. Much against the surgeon's wish was it, and all means were tried to persuade him to remain quiet. The doctor by unremitting care having succeeded in bringing the poor man round, but all was useless after the first gun was fired. The ship's boat with an awning conveyed him ten miles to Pehtang. There he mounted his horse and rode ten more to join the camp. The day was intensely hot and alas! his noble spirit, after bearing him through all fatigue, broke down during the long delay and he became much worse. Friends were with him through-out. All in the army were glad to render assistance but without avail and at last he was ordered home.

I escorted him down the river and General Napier most kindly, in conjunction with Lumsden of our regiment, did all in their power to render the transit easy. I put him on board the steamer, I thought better, but much pulled down. Alas! I little suspected his end was so fast approaching. Subsequently I have heard from a Mr Johnstone, merchant here, that your poor son wrote to him while at anchor here and that he repaired on board, and on seeing him he tried to induce him to go on shore to his house and wait till better before proceeding. But home was before him and he determined to push on. The painful end you will know and his body is beneath the deep blue sea.

To you his loss is irreparable – a nobler nature, more gallant officer or kinder friend I have never seen. You are aware that I have lived with him since my arrival in India. He taught me a soldier's duty and to his kindness I owe my position in this regiment and I mourn for him as I would for a dear brother. I trust the arrival of his brevet majority cheered his last moments. India has lost a most accomplished gallant soldier and all classes mourn for him. The papers in India have passed a high Eulogium upon him.

He left nothing with the regiment. His sword was with him. A few letters from your house have reached us and Randall and I have destroyed them according to his last wishes. Should you need for any further information or if I can aid you in any way, pray write and I shall be most happy to do all in my power.

And now dear sir, having tried poorly, I fear, but truly to express our deep loss and to ease your mind by giving you a few particulars, with earnest sympathy to you and Mrs Shebbeare,

Allow me to remain, Yours most truly,

G.A. Aufrere Baker

This is not quite the end of the China story as, unaware that Robert Shebbeare had died, Lieutenant Randall wrote him a long and interesting letter about the later actions of the 15th Punjab Regiment in the advance on Peking.

Camp Pakin, 25th October, 1860

My dear Shebbeare,

I dare say you have thought me a horrid beast for not having given all the news of our doings but really I have had little time for anything. The mail goes today and I have now only time for a mere sketch of our doings since you left. A couple of days after you went on board the despatch boat, the 1st Division marched towards Tien Tsin, which place we reached without anything worth describing. On arrival these various reports were in circulation as to what our next move was to be, but all agreed in saying that the war was at an end. I always thought, and said, it was not. After remaining in Tien Tsin for some days a small force moved on, composed chiefly of cavalry and artillery. The C-in-C and Lord Elgin also went with the force. A few days subsequently the 2nd Brigade, 1st Division, followed and, the chief party having halted at Hoosewoo, we overtook the cavalry at that place. The next day (18th September) the whole moved on, and after marching a few miles, the cavalry advance came across a picquet of the enemy's cavalry, who beat a retreat at once, but, on

121

the cavalry clearing the village in which the picquet had been posted, they found a large force of the enemy. The day before, several English and French officers had gone on to select ground for our camp as the treaty was to have been signed here. Amongst those who had gone on was Colonel Walker, and on the cavalry clearing the village back he came at a gallop with some people who had accompanied him. It was now told us that the whole of the English and French who had gone on, with the exception of Walker and those named above had been taken prisoners by Singolinski's orders, that the Chinese had thrown up earthworks and had guns in position in a semi-circle all round us, that their intention had been to allow us to encamp and then open from their guns, at the same time charging with their cavalry. This scheme had been defeated by our surprise of the advance picquet. We now formed up, the French taking the right of the road and the English the left. Sir J. Mitchell commanded the English and his general plan was to turn the enemy's right, driving them all towards their left. The Queens were to attack the village on our extreme left – the 15th the next village. For this purpose the Queens under Mitchell and Sutton marched off at once to the left village, while I was halted with skirmishers out ready to attack number two village simultaneously with the Queens. While halted, an order came from the C-in-C for regimental advance with guns and commence the attack on the enemy's centre owing to the Chinese having got our range. We therefore advanced and having driven them from the centre village, and the Chief going off with the guns and some cavalry, I brought the right shoulders forward and advanced through the town, the skirmishers working along the left of the town, supports in skirmishing order on the right, main body through the centre. On clearing the town we found about 6,000 cavalry and infantry close in front of us and all the camps standing. We drove them all before us without resistance, took all their camps (five in number) which we burned; took twenty-one guns and then, finding myself about four miles ahead of anything in the force, I halted. Everyone said the Regiment behaved admirably and I was ordered to write a despatch as I was on my own hook during the greater part of the day. I wrote plain truth and they said I had not made half enough of it – talked of Wellington, Hannibal and all sorts of rot. The chief said the Regiment skirmished splendidly without noise and in as fine order as a European Regiment. Mitchell and Sutton sang our praises and said they wished we had been with them. On the 21st we again had another go in when the Regiment was divided by wings, left wing on the left of the line fighting on the right. The enemy was fast getting round our flank when I sent to Brigadier-

General Longfield, whose guns I was supporting, to ask leave to go at them. He gave leave and we drove them off, killing several. In the evening the left wing under Harris went across the canal and attacked a large body of infantry, killing many. Chief, much pleased, called for Harris' report. We have had one man killed, 11 wounded, Baker gone away seedy after a graze on the nose. Next we advanced on Pekin itself – no opposition worth mentioning. The Summer Palace was burnt after being looted. Prize money given on the spot about £35 to subalterns; 73 DM to N.O.; 37 to Havildars; 20 to N; 13 and a half to sepoys. I have got a lot of metal said to be gold for the Regiment, if gold – about 5 or 6,000 pounds (£) – Harris has some metal equal to about £8,000 which he keeps himself. It is said we go back to India at once. The treaty was signed by the Emperor's brother yesterday. I fear the Treasure Chest money is very short but have not had time to go in to it properly yet. I think it must be at least 6,000 rupees short. I will write next mail with full particulars when I have made up the accounts. Your horse sold for 600 rupees – your traps and other description well. You shall have money in a mail or two. No more time.

Yours sincerely, Randall

Long after these events took place, Harris published his memoirs.[1] In them, he describes matters with himself in very much a central role on all occasions. He recalls his exploits mentioned above thus:

At some place on the road, called, I think, Chankiawan, where there was a fine bridge, we found the enemy in very strong force. There must have been at least 30,000 men, and we deployed to face them. Here again I found myself on the left of the line, for the General almost invariably split up my regiment into its two wings, so that I was given independent command.

Inclining my men a little to the left, we were soon completely separated from the rest of the army. Across our front was a very high and long bund, exactly like a long railway embankment, and I expect that it had something to do with the floods of the Hoang Ho river. Through this, about a mile or more ahead, there was a gap, and while making for this, I was, alongside and under the bund, three guns, each drawn by two horses tandem fashion, with some twenty-five foot-men, armed only with swords, to each gun.

I was the only mounted man of our force, so, having given Sotheby an order to bring up a couple of companies as quickly as possible, I galloped off to the gap. The Chinese, however, succeeded in getting the first gun through the gap, but I arrived in time to stop the others, and riding in front of the leading gun with a revolver in hand, I kept shouting 'Kowtow', which was the only Chinese word in my vocabulary. I do not suppose that they understood my attempt at their language, but at any rate it had the effect of making them halt. Indeed, had they moved, I intended to shoot the leading pony through the head, but they seemed quite unable to make up their minds what to do, and made no attempt to retire.

At the end of an awkward quarter of an hour my men began to struggle up at the double, and I told them to disarm all the Chinese. Had I given the order they would have killed the whole lot, but having disarmed them, I allowed them to go, and then we marched back with the guns. One of these guns was a most curious specimen. It consisted of three barrels each six feet long, and carrying a two-ounce ball, but as they could be neither elevated or depressed the gun did not seem to be of any great use outside a museum. However, it was, after all, a gun, and at the time I was mightily pleased to have captured it ... I reported to the General, and was duly complimented.'

His memoirs contain various amusing anecdotes about the campaign, of which the following is an example:

One very curious incident on this march (from Pehtang to Peking) is stamped indelibly on my memory. At a halting place the provost-marshal caught one of our 3,000 Chinese coolies in the act of looting, a thing which had been strenuously forbidden. The culprit was tried by court-marshal, and condemned to be hanged by way of example. The Chinese were drawn up on three sides of a hollow square. The scaffold was erected, and, preceded by his coffin according to the usual formula, the man was duly hanged.

But the results of this were not at all what we expected, for the whole of the Chinese coolies burst into the most uproarious laughter, and obviously considered that the whole proceeding was delightfully comical. As a spectacle they thought it first-rate, but as a deterrent it was the most dismal failure.'

The same standards did not seem to apply when it came to the British, for in the very next paragraph he continues: 'Some days after we came to a large town, called Hose-woo, and here I received my first lesson in looting, for I found myself in orders to take a hundred rank and file and loot the Government pawnbroking establishment.'

124

He went on to Peking, where, as one can see from Randall's letter, he carried out some more looting, with great success. In today's values his gold would be a fortune of several hundred thousand pounds. It was indeed customary that soldiers relied on loot, or 'prizes', to supplement their somewhat meagre salaries. What happened at Delhi, and was about to happen in China, was that the British authorities asked that prizes be pooled for distribution amongst the troops and then managed to delay paying it for years, if at all, so it is perhaps not surprising that officers did what they could for themselves.

As it was at Delhi that Robert Shebbeare chiefly distinguished himself in his short career, it is fitting that one of the Delhi soldiers should have the last word. In a letter of condolence to Robert's father, Henry Daly sums up the general feeling of loss that was felt within the army:

St Anne's Ryde, Isle of Wight, 18th November, 1860

My dear sir,

The sad announcement of the fate of your soldier son compels me to write a few words to you. My sorrow can be as nothing to your sorrow, yet perhaps you will not cast aside the deep sympathy I tender.

Intimacy prior to the days at Delhi there was none between us. At Delhi we were comrades in many trials and dangers and I learnt truly to appreciate the devotion and gallantry, the truthfulness and stoutness of your son.

I was so impressed with his merits and services that I interposed to obtain for him the command of the Guides during the last days of my incapacity from wounds; at a time when more than I can express depended on the character and bearing of the leader of the Corps.

I mourn for the loss of so good a soldier – few men of his standing possessed so much power over those under him; that is, he could and did command men. He was a rare soldier and as such he has left a name and performed services which will long be a cheering example to many in his profession.

I will not affect to write of the grief of his family, but the knowledge of the estimation in which your son was held by those who had seen him most tried may in some way soothe the parents in their affliction.

With much sympathy, believe me,

Yours faithfully, H.D. Daly

Notes

1 Harris, Major General J.T., *"China Jim" Being Incidents and Adventures in the Life of an Indian Mutiny Veteran*, Heinemann, London, 1912. History as we know it is a mixture of fact, fantasy and subjective perception, so one can be entertained by accounts of the past in the hope that much of what is said may on the whole be reasonably accurate. Despite Harris's tendency towards self-aggrandizement and Cadell's caveat (below), his memoirs are interesting in that they give yet another very personal point of view about these events.

At Delhi Harris had been with the 2nd European Fusiliers and the copy of his memoirs in the National Army Museum contains inside it a four-page original letter, dated 1912, the year of publication, from Colonel Kendal Coghill, who had been Adjutant of the Regiment, to Colonel Thomas Cadell VC, also of that Regiment, in which he systematically pours scorn on Harris's version of many events that took place before Delhi. A small sample will give the flavour:

> I have read 'China Jim' and, till now, had not known what an Angel of Light, Knowledge, and Prowess we had harboured in the old 2nd E.B.F. By his own records he is a crossbreed between an Admirable Crichton, a Baron Munchausen in piccolo and a Brigadier Gerard. More – he is a perfect economium of veracity. He has done wisely to have delayed publicising his career until all his contemporaries had passed aloft, and even himself.

MISCELLANEOUS AND SERVICE RECORD

Miscellaneous

A third cousin of Robert Shebbeare, Lieutenant Nathaniel Burslem of the 67th Regiment, was awarded a VC in the assault on the Taku Forts on 21 August 1860.

Robert Shebbeare had spent much time in dealing with the affairs of Lieutenant Murray who was killed at Delhi. The financial affairs of most officers involved something of a juggling act between income and expenditure, and after Robert's death his brother Henry had to sort many complications out. There is much correspondence about it all, of which the following letter from Lieutenant Baker to Henry is a typical example. Letter to Henry Shebbeare (Robert Shebbeare's brother) from Lieutenant Baker:

Benares, March 9th, 1861. We march for Jullundhur

My dear Shebbeare,

I regret exceedingly having lost a mail ere replying to yours that duly reached me at Calcutta, but I have been very ill ever since the taking of Pekin and was very nearly forced to re-visit England the other day. I am now better and am travelling up towards the Punjab where the Regiment is going to be cantoned; the exact station as yet I know not. Your letter I have unfortunately packed up and it is not by my side to refer to, but to the best of my ability I will answer you questions and give you all the information I possess relative to your lamented brother with regard to his personal estate.

I think I can say that your brother lived fully up to his income and had never saved money. Indeed, so liberal and open-handed was he that the reverse may be expected. If it is so, his life was insured and that would cover his debts. His heavy baggage was sold at his own request when leaving China and fetched a good sum and I bought his horse for £85.0.0. Randall has the account but perhaps deductions will have to be made for mess expenses.

Your brother owned a house also in Umballa, but what has become of it during the last three years I know not, and if still in repair. I fear no purchaser would be found in these days who would give an eighth of its value. I shall make enquiries and inspect the house as I pass through. I also have not been able to solve the question regarding the payment of his passage money to England. I know he procured a Draft from the commissariat for the amount, but I received a letter from the poor fellow dated Hong Kong, saying he had lost the draft and wanted me to procure a duplicate. This I was unable to do, and unless he subsequently found the draft I do not think he had sufficient to pay the large sum required for the passage. If paid, half of it at least should be refunded.

The documents relating to the transfer of prize money hold good. They were bought by your brother from the several parties, Wolseley, Ward, Elton etc for ready cash, and in the distribution of prize, will have to be paid to the estate.

I visited the 'Emeu' at Singapore and was shown the Log Book, and I conveyed you and my own thanks to the Captain for his kindness to your poor brother in giving up his cabin entirely to him, and personally seeing he wanted for nothing. Being on service at the time no committee of adjustment could be formed but now there is one. They have to collect all particulars with regard to his estate and sell all property, sending the money to government, who pay such claims as appear consistent, and then publish in the Gazette the amount of assets. This will take some months.

I trust my previous letter to Mr Shebbeare was duly received. It was a heavy blow indeed to all, to you doubly so.

He was greatly beloved by all who knew him, and the regiment adored him.

The picture, or rather portraits, of Randall were your brother's property.

With very kind regards to you and Mrs Shebbeare. Believe me, sincerely yours,

G. Aufrere Baker

Lieutenant Baker's records show that he was on leave at Simla when the 60th mutinied at Rohtuck. On return he was posted to

Delhi where he did duty with Hodson's Horse, becoming Adjutant in February 1858, and he saw action at Rohundshuker, Allygurt, Futtepore Seekre, Mynpoorie and the final capture of Lucknow. He took part in field operations in Oudh in 1858 and saw further actions at Nawabgung and Fyzabad. Medal and two clasps. Honourable mention in despatches.

He volunteered for the China Expedition (at Robert Shebbeare's request) and was at Pehtang, Sinho and the Taku Forts. Actions at Hoosewoo and Chunkiakan. Twice honourably mentioned in despatches and a medal with two clasps. On return to India he joined the 8th Hussars and then became Adjutant of the 6th Bengal Cavalry, in which regiment he was in 1864.

Robert Shebbeare's Service Record

Joined 60th Bengal Native Infantry in 1844. Ensign, 29 February 1844. Lieutenant, 15 November 1849. Officiating Interpreter and Quartermaster of the Regiment, from 1852. Adjutant, 16 January 1854. Adjutant, Interpreter and Quartermaster, February 1855. Escaped with Colonel Seaton from 60th, which mutinied at Rohtuck. ADC to Brigadier Showers, Delhi, 1857 – saw several 'sharp actions' with him (3 days). Appointed to Guide Corps (Second in Command and acting Commandant). On duty at Hindoo Rao's and other hotspots, June–September). Victoria Cross on 14 September 1857 at Kichengunge, Delhi. Offered Second in Command of Hodson's Horse and Coke's Rifles, but in October 1857 was asked by General Chamberlain to raise a new Regiment, 15th Punjab Infantry (later 23rd Sikh Pioneers). 3rd Battalion volunteered for wars in China, 1860. Brevet Major.

Captain Knollys, in *The Victoria Cross in India* says of Robert Shebbeare's exploits:

On the 14th September, 1857, the day of the assault of Delhi, Captain R.H. Shebbeare commanded the detachment of the Guides forming part of Reid's column. Through want of guns, the weakness of the force and the absence of steadiness on the part of the Cashmere contingent, as well as the strong position of the enemy, who much outnumbered their opponents, the operations were a failure. The Goorkhas, the Guides and the men of the 60th Rifles, however, fought well. An endeavour was made to storm a large loopholed courtyard. Twice Captain Shebbeare charged up to the wall; twice were the stormers driven back. He retired to organize a third attack but one third of the Europeans and many of our native soldiers having failed, he was obliged to abandon the attempt. He then collected some men and covered the retreat of the column. He came out of action with a bullet through his cheek and a bad scalp wound from another bullet. He received the Victoria Cross for his gallantry. Captain Shebbeare repeatedly distinguished himself throughout the mutiny. We regret to add that his name is no longer to be found in the Army List.

Robert's parents lived in Surbiton and a stained-glass window in his memory was installed in St Mark's Church, but was unfortunately destroyed by a bomb during the Second World War.

THE SHEBBEARE FAMILY

This short history has been included, as an 'optional extra', chiefly to give the reader some idea of the background of the family in which Robert Shebbeare was brought up; but it is also intended that by following some threads through to almost recent times, his descendants may find enthusiasm to delve into the large amount of material that is yet to be explored in the Devon Record Office. As many of the previous family genealogists seemed to have concentrated on the males and the male lines, there is perhaps a lot of scope to research the many admirable women who feature in the family, and also to bring the family history up to date with details of the current generations.

Shebbeare is a family that originated in Devon, and over the generations it has produced many distinguished soldiers, sailors, lawyers and churchmen. Early Shebbeares lived at Shebbeare Town in the parish of Abbotsham in North Devon during the sixteenth century, and on the flyleaf of the seventeenth-century family Bible of Richard Shebbeare is recorded: 'My great-grandfather new-built the parlour at Shebbeare Town about 1580.' In the seventeenth century a branch moved to Okehampton where members took a prominent part in the life of the town, two of them being mayors of the borough. During his term of office, one of these kept an account book in which he also recorded events in the town, and this, 'Richard Shebbeare's Booke, 1669' is now in the Devon Record Office.

The best-known early member of the family was Dr John Shebbeare. Born at Shebbeare Town in 1710 he was educated at the Grammar School in Exeter under Zachariah Mudge and showed signs of early literary promise. He was apprenticed to a surgeon in Exeter at the age of sixteen but having lampooned his master and members of the Corporation he moved to Bristol and set up in partnership with a chemist. In 1740 he published a book called *A New Analysis of the Bristol Water together with the Cause of Diabetes and Hectic and their Cure as it results from these Waters*. It seems just possible that he and his partner were in business selling the water at the time!

In 1752 he moved to Paris where he took a medical degree, became a member of the Academy of Science and was apparently awarded a doctorate in medicine. He returned to England via Jersey, where he wrote a history of the island, and settled in London in 1754 as a political writer. He wrote a novel, *The Marriage Act*, opposing Lord Hardwicke's marriage reforms. His thirty-four published works include plays, novels, satirical, political, historical and medical works but his best-known work is *Letters to the People of England*, which was designed to show that the grandeur of France and the misfortunes of England were entirely due to the House of Hanover being on the throne of England. As a consequence, the Attorney-General filed an information against him and he was found guilty of libel, for which he was sentenced to pay a fine of £5, stand one hour in the pillory at Charing Cross and suffer three years' imprisonment. He was driven in a coach provided by Under-Sheriff Beardmore to Charing Cross, where the latter's kindly chairman held an umbrella over his head to shelter him from the elements, the first time that this novelty was used in public in England. He went to prison for some time, but was later awarded a pension by the King, in order to keep him quiet, it is thought.

He obviously raised strong and different emotions in people. Chambers *Book of Days* says: 'He died at a good old age in 1788, greatly lamented by his friends, for this Ishmael of politics and public life is represented a very amiable and worthy man in all his private relations, as husband, son, father, brother and friend.' The 22-year-old Fanny Burney, on the other hand, in her diary (1774), spent an evening in his company and noted:

> He absolutely ruined our evening; for he is the most morose, rude, gross and ill-mannered man I was ever in company with. He aims perpetually at wit, though he constantly stops short at rudeness ... What most incited his spleen was Woman, to whom he professes a fixed aversion; and next to this his greatest disgust is against the Scotch; and these two subjects he wore threadbare ... The only novelty which they owed to him was his extraordinary coarseness of language he made use of.

Her companion thought that the old doctor had his reputation for misanthropy to keep up, and was doubtless trying to shock her. Fanny mentions later that 'Miss Reid was, I suppose, somewhat scandalised at the man's conversation, as it happened in her house, and therefore, before we took leave, she said, "Now I must tell you that Dr Shebbeare has only been jesting; he thinks as we do all the time."'

Opinion as to his literary talents seems to have been divided too. Macaulay called him 'a wretched scribbler', while Dr Johnson said, 'He had knowledge and abilities much above the class of ordinary writers and deserves to be remembered as a respectable name in literature were it only for his admirable "Letters on the English Nation".'

Like him or loathe him, he obviously made his mark on society at the time. Dr John had one son, the Rev. John Shebbeare, Rector of East Hornden in Essex, who was a bachelor and a noted musician. His younger brother Joseph had a son, Charles, who became a doctor, and he in turn produced Charles John, Robert Haydon's father. There is a family portrait of Charles John Shebbeare which was done in pastel by William Russell, son of John Russell RA, the well-known artist, who was himself very talented and might have outshone his father had he not gone into the Church. He was a neighbour of the Shebbeares near Guildford.

Charles John Shebbeare became a solicitor and then at the age of forty or so, sent himself up to Queen's College, Cambridge as a Fellow Commoner. He was later called to the Bar and set up in chambers at 5, New Square, Lincoln's Inn. He married Louisa Matilda Wolfe, aged sixteen, daughter of the Rev. Robert Barbor Wolfe. After the Treaty of Amiens in 1802, the Reverend Robert had decided to take his family for a holiday to the Continent and was in France when in 1803, Napoleon, against all international agreements at the time, ordered that every English person be detained and held prisoner. His book, *The English Prisoners in France*, published in 1830, was an account of his experiences as chaplain to the English community at Givet and Verdun from 1803 to 1812. Louisa herself wrote 'A Childhood in France' for her family, and in it she describes seeing Napoleon sitting on a table, swinging his legs to and fro and throwing bon-bons into the air, which he caught in his mouth. Louisa's brother, Henry, became a Captain in the Honourable East India Company's service and compiled a scrapbook of drawings of his voyages in the 1820s–1840s, an edited version of which is to be published in due course.

Charles and Louisa had ten children, two of whom died in infancy:

Charles Hooper (1824–1887), Rector of Wykeham in Yorkshire; Robert Haydon (1827–1860) VC; Henry Francis, 'Harry' (1828–1897), barrister; Margaretta Louisa, 'Peggy' (1831–1873), married Charles Govett; Emma Jane, 'Joan' (1832–1908); Helen Charlotte, 'Nelly' (1834–1922), married William Bennett; Reginald John, 'Jack' (1839–1916); and Alice Mary (1844-1922), unmarried, became a sister at Holy Cross Convent.

The Shebbeare archive includes a large number of family photographs dating from the late 1850s onwards and the illustrations of Robert Haydon's parents and siblings are all from that source.

The Rev. Charles Hooper Shebbeare and his wife Lucy Marian (née Inge) brought up a large family of nine children and, in order to educate them from his small stipend, they had to forgo many luxuries. Charles Hooper is said to have taken two holidays in thirty-four years, and on the second he caught a chill from which he died – an object lesson on the dangers of excess perhaps!

His eldest son, the Rev. Charles John Shebbeare DD was a priest and theologian of high repute, with many books to his credit, including *The Greek Theory of the State*, *The Problem of the Future Life*, *Religion in an Age of Doubt* and *The Challenge of the Universe*: all topics which continue to occupy us today. He was Rector at Swerford in Oxfordshire before moving to a sixteen-bedroom rectory at Stanhope in County Durham. Robert Inge Shebbeare tells me that there was a central-heating system which was lit with much ceremony when they arrived, but after a week, in which a ton of coke was consumed and a gardener called Briggs constantly employed to stoke the monster, it was never used again! He held theological lectureships at both Oxford and Cambridge, and in 1921 he was appointed a Chaplain to the King, travelling down once a year to preach at the Chapel Royal. In 1930 he prepared a sermon in defence of foxhunting but on the day he decided that this would be an inappropriate subject as the R.101 disaster had just occurred, so he published it instead, and received many letters of criticism. About the same time also he accepted the mastership of the local hunt which drew more correspondence, not least from the Bishop of Durham, Herbert Hensley Henson, who wrote, apropos of going to heaven: 'Will the Master of the Wear Valley Beagles have the endless felicity of meeting again not only his well-loved hounds but also the hares which they, and he, delighted to hunt? I am content to remain an agnostic.' Charles John's wife Evelyne (née Joyce) continued the family habit of keeping all her correspondence and through her three sons' letters to her we can trace their interesting lives as they unfold. Robert Inge Shebbeare's first literary offering, for instance, gets straight to the point and reads, 'Dear Santa. Eeyore or stilts.'

Their eldest son, William Godolphin Conway ('Bill') Shebbeare, deserves some special mention. After Winchester, he went up to Christ Church, Oxford, where he became a committed Socialist and in 1936 was elected President of the Oxford Union, ahead of Max Beloff. He became a leader writer for the *Daily Herald* and at the age of twenty-four was elected to the predominantly Conservative Council in Holborn. His political career was cut short by the war when he enlisted in the Army. He wrote a book called *A Soldier looks Ahead* under the pen name of 'Captain X', which contained many interesting ideas for the future of the Army. While he was leading his squadron into action at the battle for Caen in Normandy his tank was hit and, because there had been a report that he had been seen in a dazed state afterwards, he was posted as missing. His parents spent a long and distressing time interviewing survivors from his regiment, the 23rd Hussars, in the hope of finding that he had perhaps been taken prisoner, but after a whole year it was confirmed that he had been killed in action. Many years later a member of the family met Prime Minister Harold Wilson, who, on learning that he was a relation of Bill Shebbeare, said, 'If he'd been alive today, he'd have had my job.'

Robert Austin Shebbeare fought in the First World War and was awarded the DSO and the Croix de Guerre. His eldest son Charles Charlewood has descendants, Owain and Rupert, who live in Melbourne, Australia.

His younger son, also Robert Austin, joined the Guides Cavalry in 1930 and noted in his memoirs that in the Mess at the Guides Headquarters at Mardan there was one leaf of a mahogany table taken from Hindoo Rao's House after the Siege of Delhi and leaves had been added on to form a table to seat forty. The other two leaves were taken by the 60th Rifles and the Sirmoor Battalion of Gurkhas, who also fought alongside the Guides on the ridge; each leaf had crests and mottoes carved on them, 'Rough and Ready' in the case of the Guides. Later, as ADC to the Governor of Sind, Sir Lancelot Graham, he travelled with him around the province on tours of inspection. One morning, the train made an early stop for breakfast and Sir Lancelot, still clad in curious night apparel consisting of a sort of smock, shorts like a Chinaman, together with a cummerbund, decided to take a short walk up the line, leaving unseen on the non-platform side. He returned to see the train receding into the disance without him and said to the stationmaster, 'I am the Governor of Sind and that is my train,' to which came the quick retort, 'Yes, and I am the Queen of Sheba.' Sir Lancelot was eventually reunited with his transport and Robert Austin later married his daughter, Frances. Robert Austin was commanding the 3rd Indian Grenadiers at the time of partition in 1947. While extricating his regiment by train from Pakistan it was attacked by a large number of hostile tribesmen and he was wounded. His young daughter, Jenny, who was about five at the time, shouted out, 'Don't let these nasty men steal our lunch!' He was awarded the Shaurya Chakra, an Indian decoration for gallantry which is given 'for valour, courageous action or self-sacrifice away from the battlefield'.

One of his sons, Antony, lives in Canada and the other, Sir Tom Shebbeare, is well known today as the former Chief Executive of the Prince's Trust and present Director of the Prince's Charities.

Edward Oswald Shebbeare, 'Ned,' the youngest son, joined the Indian Forest Service in 1906 and in 1938, having retired as Chief Conservator of Forests in Bengal, he took a job as Chief Game Warden in Malaya, where he set up the King George V National Park near Kuala Lumpur. At the outbreak of war he was sent to Singapore to train troops in jungle warfare, was captured by the Japanese and spent three and a half years as a PoW. He was a member of the 1924 and 1933 Everest Expeditions, being second in command of the latter, and was a well-known writer on Indian topics. His delightful book about an elephant that he had known for thirty-five years, *Soondar Mooni*, is still very popular.

Charles Hooper Shebbeare also had five daughters, all strong characters, none of whom married. Ursula Katherine ('Kitty') was for many years a missionary in China, while Margaret ran her own nursing home and started a club for nurses in Cavendish Square. Hilda was connected with nursing also and Monica worked in a bank, which was rather unusual at the time. Two of them, Mary and Margaret, lived later in Scarborough with their brother, Laurence Robert Inge ('Bill'), who had been badly injured in the First World War. These two 'Scarborough Aunts' were very strict, in a nice way, and had very clear house rules that young members of the family rather appreciated, as they said that 'they knew where they stood' when they went to stay.

Henry Francis ('Harry') Shebbeare went up to Trinity College, Cambridge, and practised as a barrister in his father's chambers. He married a cousin, Lily Lucy Roberta Wolfe, by whom he had four children. Lucy was unmarried and Celia, who was a nursing sister in the First World War, married a classical scholar and writer, Denis Turner; Henry Vivian was an architect and a talented artist in oils and watercolours, who exhibited in London from 1920 to 1960; Francis Wolfe fought in the First World War and in 1917 wrote a letter to Celia which ends: 'I am at the moment living in a very nice farmhouse, and the country is looking its best. I shall be going up the line again shortly, and its getting a bit hot up there now.' He was shot in both legs and wounded severely at La Vacquerie where he was serving with the Machine Gun Corps, and invalided home. He continued the Family Book started by Henry Francis and married a glamorous actress called Maritza ('Betty'), daughter of Sir Harry and Lady Lowndes.

Reginald John ('Jack') Shebbeare worked for forty-three years at Somerset House, where he became a Principal Clerk, and had four children. Two of the sons, Ernest Reginald and Wilfred George, became priests. The former was one of the Brighton clergymen who left the Church of England in 1910 and converted to Roman Catholicism. He was priest at Woodbridge in Suffolk and rebuilt the church there to his own design. The latter became Dom Alphege Shebbeare OSB, and was a noted musician who taught at Downside. Claude Eustace Shebbeare, following the family tradition, became a barrister in his uncle's chambers; he was keenly interested in genealogy and heraldry and was the father of Mary Lamb, who has been so kind in supplying information about the family.

Sources
Family Bibles, correspondence, wills, deeds, parish registers, family books and memoirs, notes for a talk to the Okehampton History Society by the late Major J.D. Shebbeare, and information supplied by Robert Inge Shebbeare and Mary Lamb.

John Govett LVO, a descendant of Margaretta Louisa Shebbeare, has kindly provided a selective Shebbeare family tree. Apologies to the members of the many ancillary lines whose names, for lack of space, do not appear, but space has been left below the Family Tree for further handwritten additions.

Line from Shebbeares

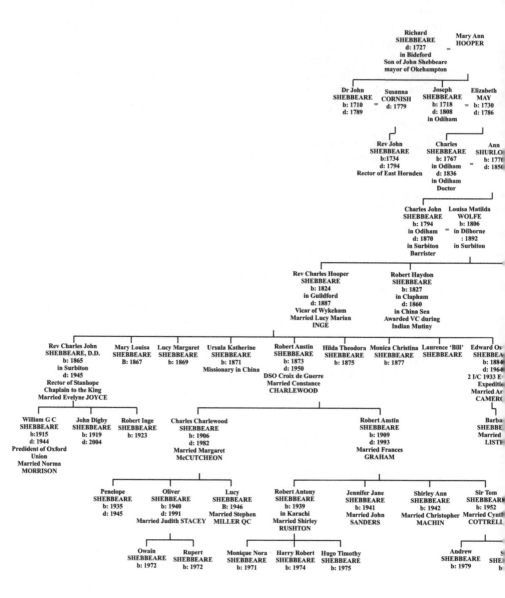

Richard SHEBBEARE d: 1727 in Bideford Son of John Shebbeare mayor of Okehampton = Mary Ann HOOPER

Dr John SHEBBEARE b: 1710 d: 1789 = Susanna CORNISH d: 1779

Joseph SHEBBEARE b: 1718 d: 1808 in Odiham = Elizabeth MAY b: 1730 d: 1786

Rev John SHEBBEARE b:1734 d: 1794 Rector of East Hornden

Charles SHEBBEARE b: 1767 in Odiham d: 1836 in Odiham Doctor = Ann SHURLO b: 1770 d: 1850

Charles John SHEBBEARE b: 1794 in Odiham d: 1870 in Surbiton Barrister = Louisa Matilda WOLFE b: 1806 in Dilhorne : 1892 in Surbiton

Rev Charles Hooper SHEBBEARE b: 1824 in Guildford d: 1887 Vicar of Wykeham Married Lucy Marian INGE

Robert Haydon SHEBBEARE b: 1827 in Clapham d: 1860 in China Sea Awarded VC during Indian Mutiny

Rev Charles John SHEBBEARE, D.D. b: 1865 in Surbiton d: 1945 Rector of Stanhope Chaplain to the King Married Evelyne JOYCE

Mary Louisa SHEBBEARE B: 1867

Lucy Margaret SHEBBEARE b: 1869

Ursula Katherine SHEBBEARE b: 1871 Missionary in China

Robert Austin SHEBBEARE b: 1873 d: 1950 DSO Croix de Guerre Married Constance CHARLEWOOD

Hilda Theodora SHEBBEARE b: 1875

Monica Christina SHEBBEARE b: 1877

Laurence 'Bill' SHEBBEARE

Edward Os SHEBBEA b: 1884 d: 1964 2 I/C 1933 E Expediti Married Ar CAMER(

William G C SHEBBEARE b:1915 d: 1944 Predident of Oxford Union Married Norma MORRISON

John Digby SHEBBEARE b: 1919 d: 2004

Robert Inge SHEBBEARE b: 1923

Charles Charlewood SHEBBEARE b: 1906 d: 1982 Married Margaret McCUTCHEON

Robert Austin SHEBBEARE b: 1909 d: 1993 Married Frances GRAHAM

Barba SHEBBE Married LISTE

Penelope SHEBBEARE b: 1935 d: 1945

Oliver SHEBBEARE b: 1940 d: 1991 Married Judith STACEY

Lucy SHEBBEARE B: 1946 Married Stephen MILLER QC

Robert Antony SHEBBEARE b: 1939 in Karachi Married Shirley RUSHTON

Jennifer Jane SHEBBEARE b: 1941 Married John SANDERS

Shirley Ann SHEBBEARE b: 1942 Married Christopher MACHIN

Sir Tom SHEBBEAR b: 1952 Married Cynt COTTRELL

Owain SHEBBEARE b: 1972

Rupert SHEBBEARE b: 1972

Monique Nora SHEBBEARE b: 1971

Harry Robert SHEBBEARE b: 1974

Hugo Timothy SHEBBEARE b: 1975

Andrew SHEBBEARE b: 1979

S SHE b:

SHEBBEARE

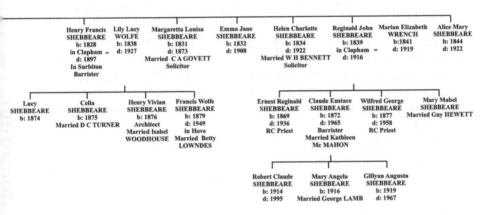

Henry Francis SHEBBEARE	Lily Lucy WOLFE	Margaretta Louisa SHEBBEARE	Emma Jane SHEBBEARE	Helen Charlotte SHEBBEARE	Reginald John SHEBBEARE	Marian Elizabeth WRENCH	Alice Mary SHEBBEARE
b: 1828 in Clapham = d: 1897 In Surbiton Barrister	b: 1838 d: 1927	b: 1831 d: 1873 Married C A GOVETT Solicitor	b: 1832 d: 1908	b: 1834 d: 1922 Married W H BENNETT Solicitor	b: 1839 in Clapham = d: 1916	b:1841 d: 1919	b: 1844 d: 1922

Lucy SHEBBEARE	Celia SHEBBEARE	Henry Vivian SHEBBEARE	Francis Wolfe SHEBBEARE		Ernest Reginald SHEBBEARE	Claude Eustace SHEBBEARE	Wilfred George SHEBBEARE	Mary Mabel SHEBBEARE
b: 1874	b: 1875 Married D C TURNER	b: 1876 Architect Married Isabel WOODHOUSE	b: 1879 d: 1949 in Hove Married Betty LOWNDES		b: 1869 d: 1936 RC Priest	b: 1872 d: 1965 Barrister Married Kathleen Mc MAHON	b: 1877 d: 1958 RC Priest	Married Guy HEWETT

Robert Claude SHEBBEARE	Mary Angela SHEBBEARE	Gillyan Augusta SHEBBEARE
b: 1914 d: 1995	b: 1916 Married George LAMB	b: 1919 d: 1967

BIBLIOGRAPHY

An Officer Who Served There, *History of the Siege of Delhi*, Adam and Charles Black, Edinburgh, 1861.

David, Saul, *The Indian Mutiny, 1857*, Viking, London, 2002. An excellent, well-researched and interesting book, on which I have much relied in making the brief introductions to the chapters.

Daly, General Sir Henry Dermot, *Memoirs of Sir Henry Dermot*, 1905.

Entract, J.P., 'Riddell's Record of the 60th Regiment of Bengal Native Infantry: With a Sequel on the 3rd Europeans'. In *Journal of the Society for Army Historical Research*, War Office, 1964.

Harris, Major General J.T., *'China Jim' Being Incidents and Adventures in the Life of an Indian Mutiny Veteran*, Heinemann, London, 1912.

Hibbert, Christopher, *The Great Mutiny; India 1857*, London, 1980.

Hodson, G.H., *Twelve Years of a Soldier's Life in India: Being Extracts from the Letters of the Late Major W.S.R. Hodson*, London, 1859.

Jackson, Major Donovan, *India's Army*, Sampson Low, Marston and Co. Ltd., London, 1940.

Khan, Sir Syed Ahmad, *The Causes of Indian Revolt (1857)*, Lahore, 1873.

Knollys, Captain, *The Victoria Cross in India*, London, 1876.

Lumsden, P.S. and Elmsmie, G.R., *Lumsden of the Guides*, London, 1899.

McCrumm, Lieutenant General Sir George, *History of the Guides, 1846–1922*, Gale and Polden Ltd, Aldershot, 1938.

Mason, Philip, *A Matter of Honour: An Account of the Indian Army. Its Officers and Men*, Jonathan Cape, London, 1974.

Norman, Major H.W., *A Narrative of the Campaign of the Delhi Army*, W.H. Dalton, London, 1858.

——, Field Marshal Sir Henry Wylie, *Memoirs of Field Marshal Sir Henry Wylie Norman*, London, 1908.

Pearson, Hesketh, *The Hero of Delhi*, Penguin, London, 1939.

Reid, General Sir Charles, GCB, *Extracts from letters and notes written down during the Siege of Delhi in 1857*, Henry S. King, London.

Rotton, John E.W., *The Chaplain's Narrative of the Siege of Delhi*, London, 1858 and Blackett, London, 1866.

Russell, William Howard, *My Indian Mutiny Diary*, edited by Michael Edwardes, Cassell and Co. Ltd., London, 1957.

Seaton, Major General Sir Thomas, KCB, *From Cadet to Colonel. The Record of a Life of Active Service*, Hurst and Blackett, London, 1866.

Shebbeare, Family Papers. Letters home from Major Robert Haydon Shebbeare. Memo book, 1855–6 (when Adjutant of 60th NI). Diary, 1860. Correspondence concerning the effects and affairs of the late Lt Alexander Murray, attached to the Guides, killed at Kissengunge. Miscellaneous administrative records of the 15th Punjab Regiment. Letters of condolence to Charles John Shebbeare. Correspondence concerning the financial affairs of Major Robert Shebbeare after his death. Letters to Robert Shebbeare from Messrs Reid, Seaton, Muter and Daly. Orders from Hindoo Rao's Picquet.

Toomey, T.E., *Heroes of the Victoria Cross*, George Newnes Ltd, London, 1895.

Walker, Colonel T.N., *Through the Mutiny. Reminiscences of 30 Years Active Service and Sport in India (1854–66)*, Gibbings and Co., London, 1907.

Wilson, Major General Archdale, Correspondence, National Army Museum.

INDEX

142

143

Military Units